The Original Jesus

FRONT COVER AND FACING PAGE:
Detail from a wall-painting in the fourth-century catacomb of Commodilla, near Rome, depicting Christ in majesty. The Greek letters in the background are an allusion to the description of Jesus as 'the Alpha and Omega, the first and the last, the beginning and the end' in the book of Revelation *(22:13)*.

The Original Jesus

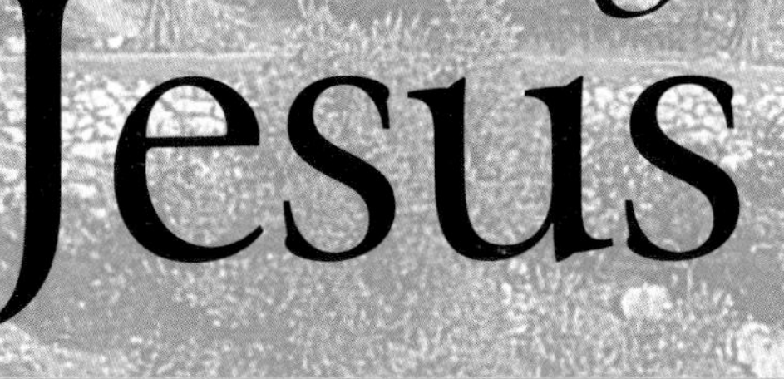

The Life and Vision of a Revolutionary

Tom Wright

A LION BOOK

Published by
Lion Publishing plc
Sandy Lane West, Oxford, England
ISBN 0 7459 3801 9
Albatross Books Pty Ltd
PO Box 320, Sutherland, NSW 2232, Australia
ISBN 0 7324 1705 8

First hardback edition 1996
First paperback edition 1997
10 9 8 7 6 5 4 3 2 1 0

Acknowledgments
Scripture quotations taken from the HOLY BIBLE, NEW INTERNATIONAL VERSION. Copyright © 1973, 1978, 1984 by International Bible Society. Used by permission of Hodder & Stoughton Ltd. All rights reserved: pages 2, 117, 133.
Scripture text marked NRSV is from the New Revised Standard Version of the Bible, copyright © 1989 by the Division of Christian Education of the National Council of the Churches of Christ in the USA: pages 10–11, 15, 22, 23, 27, 32, 34–36, 38, 44–46, 50, 53, 56, 64, 86, 94–95, 118, 134, 138, 139.

A catalogue record for this book is available
from the British Library

Printed and bound in Spain

Contents

Preface

Jesus is as much in the news now as ever before.

An archaeologist digs up a new stone; an archivist redates a manuscript; a seminar comes up with a new analysis; and suddenly the newspapers get interested. Does this new view 'mean' that Jesus never did or said what the Gospels say he did or said? Or perhaps that, after all, he really did? The passion these questions arouse shows that a lot of people are still fascinated by Jesus—even if they sometimes hope to find a rather different Jesus from the one in the biblical Gospels.

When the BBC invited me to film a sequence of programmes about Jesus, as part of their 'First Light' series, it was a wonderful challenge. I was in the middle of writing a serious scholarly book on Jesus, and had to change gear for a week and speak as simply and directly as I could, in non-technical language. I have nothing but praise for the producer, Graham Judd, the director, Bethwyn Serow, who set the series up and helped in so many ways, and for the cameraman, Geoff Kay, and the sound engineer, Steve Robertshaw, who travelled round Israel with us for a week and did the actual hard work.

I have expanded the text a little. The first half of the book is a slightly fuller version of what appeared on television. The second half was added so that people who were intrigued by the first half could see how they might follow the issues up and begin to find out more for themselves. Here my gratitude goes particularly to Philip Law and his colleagues at Lion Publishing, for their enthusiasm and willingness to work at speed to help bring the book to birth.

At every point I am fully aware of the need to explain things in more detail, and to argue for my own interpretations. This I have done in various places, notably *The New Testament and the People of God* (1992), and *Jesus and the Victory of God* (which should be published around the same time as the present volume). Both books are published by SPCK in London, and Fortress Press in Minneapolis. There is no doubt much more to be said, but those books represent, I hope, a couple of steps in the right direction.

It only remains to thank my colleagues at Lichfield Cathedral for coping during my absences, both in Israel while filming and in my study while writing and rewriting; and, yet again, to thank my dear wife and children for their patience, support and love.

Tom Wright
Lichfield Cathedral
Pentecost 1996

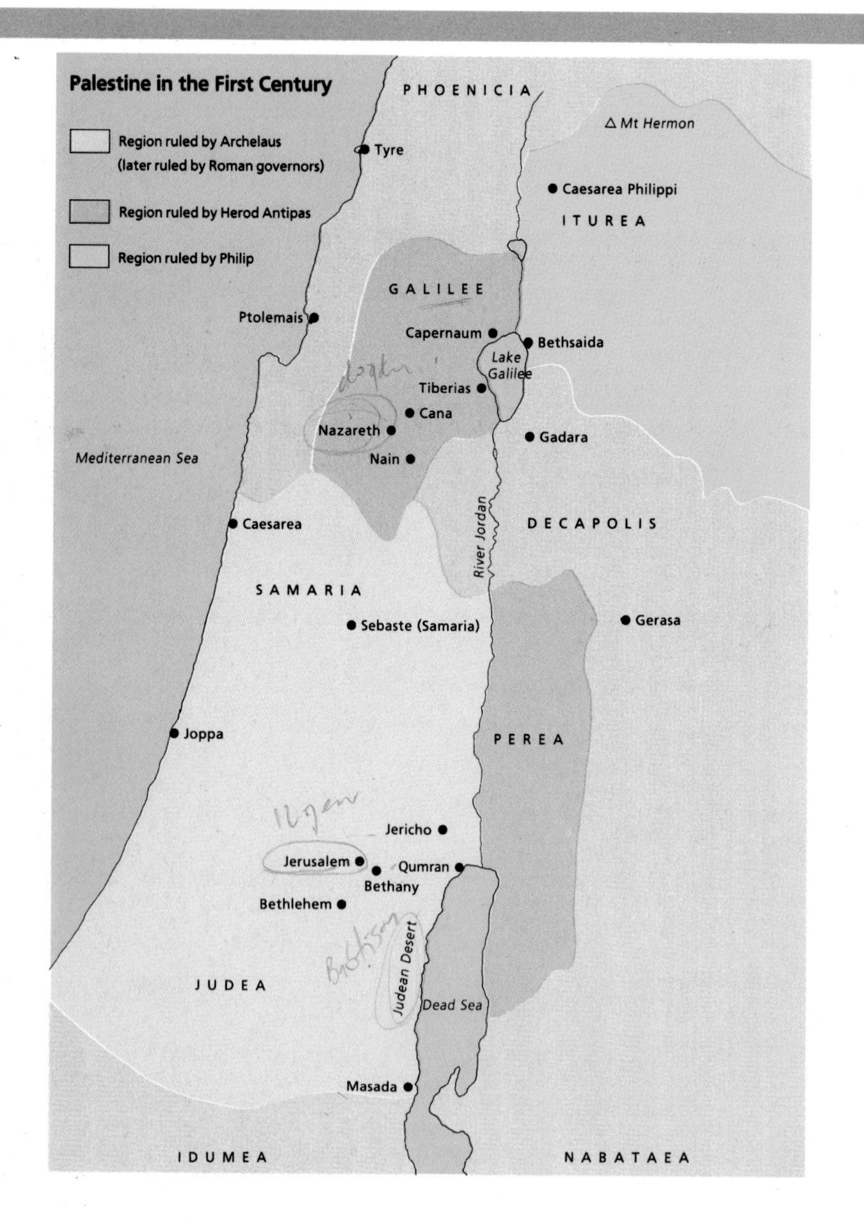
Palestine in the First Century
Region ruled by Archelaus (later ruled by Roman governors)
Region ruled by Herod Antipas
Region ruled by Philip
PHOENICIA
Mt Hermon
Tyre
Caesarea Philippi
ITUREA
GALILEE
Ptolemais
Capernaum
Bethsaida
Lake Galilee
Tiberias
Cana
Nazareth
Gadara
Nain
Mediterranean Sea
Caesarea
DECAPOLIS
River Jordan
SAMARIA
Sebaste (Samaria)
Gerasa
Joppa
PEREA
Jericho
Jerusalem
Qumran
Bethany
Bethlehem
Judean Desert
JUDEA
Dead Sea
Masada
IDUMEA
NABATAEA

Part 1

Jesus– Then and Now

1

The End of a Beautiful Dream

It was nine o'clock in the morning when they crucified him. The inscription of the charge against him read, 'The King of the Jews'. And with him they crucified two bandits, one on his right and one on his left. [And the scripture was fulfilled that says, 'And he was counted among the lawless.'] Those who passed by derided him, shaking their heads and saying, 'Aha! You who would destroy the temple and build it in three days, save yourself, and come down from the cross!' In the same way the chief priests, along with the scribes, were also mocking him among themselves and saying, 'He saved others; he cannot save himself. Let the Messiah, the King of Israel, come down from the cross now, so that we may see and believe.' Those who were crucified with him also taunted him.

When it was noon, darkness came over the whole land until three in the afternoon. At three o'clock Jesus cried out with a loud voice, 'Eloi, Eloi, lema sabachthani?' which means, 'My God, my God, why have you forsaken me?'

MARK 15:25–34

You don't have to walk down too many streets in Jerusalem before you realize: this place is different. Not just different like, say, New York is different from York, or Los Angeles is different from Leicester. It may or may not be true, as the old hymn says, that 'the hopes and fears of all the years' were met together in Bethlehem on Christmas Eve. But it's certainly true that the pain and the tears of all the years meet together here in Jerusalem, just a few miles north of Bethlehem. You can feel it as you walk around. You can see it in the faces you meet. You can hear it on the edge of every conversation. If you shut out for a few minutes the camels and the cameras, the tacky tourist shops and the relentless religion, you may discover it in yourself.

The first time I came to Jerusalem, I found myself overwhelmed by it. I had a strange sense that, somehow, the magic and madness of the whole world, the joy and the pain of the whole human race, were locked together in that city. And I found that all the pain that I knew about—in myself, and in the rest of the world—seemed to be focussed right there, drawing together the shocking events of the first century

PREVIOUS PAGE: Jerusalem, conquered and made the capital of Israel by King David around 1000 BC, had been occupied by the Romans for half a century by the time Jesus was born. The Temple Mount—the sacred site on which King Solomon built the first temple—is now occupied by the Islamic Dome of the Rock (centre left).

and the raw pain of the twentieth, as well as all the messy and muddled bits in between.

Jerusalem is the place where the glory and the folly of the world is concentrated. It is where the joy and the pain of the human race come together, the irresistible force and the immovable object. And, although the story of Jesus starts a

The people who crowded through the narrow streets of Jerusalem nearly two thousand years ago were expecting God's Messiah, or 'anointed one', to overthrow the occupying Roman forces and lead Israel back to freedom.

The Jewish people have always believed that the God they worshipped was the one true God of all the earth...

Thus says the Lord, the King of Israel,
 and his Redeemer, the Lord of hosts:
I am the first and I am the last;
 besides me there is no god.
Who is like me? Let them proclaim it,
 let them declare and set it forth before me.

I made the earth,
 and created humankind upon it;
it was my hands that stretched out the heavens,
 and I commanded all their host.

ISAIAH 44:6–7; 45:12

few miles down the road, in Bethlehem, this is where it all led to. Jerusalem is the place where Jesus came: to celebrate, and to die.

So what?

Puzzled people in the modern Western world often ask: how can the death of a man 2,000 years ago, in another culture and another place, be relevant for me, at this end of the twentieth century? And it does seem bizarre to suggest that something of universal importance could happen at one place and at one time, rather than being a general truth, hanging in the air over the whole world at once. But that's a very un-Jewish question; it is, so to speak, a very un-Jerusalem question.

Puzzled people in the modern Western world often ask: how can the death of a man 2,000 years ago, in another culture and another place, be relevant for me, at this end of the twentieth century?

The point is, the Jewish people have always believed that the God they worshipped was the one true God of all the earth; so what happened close up, in their own history, was seen to be of universal importance. And when you stand in the streets of Jerusalem, it doesn't seem such a silly idea. This place, according to the Bible, was where Abraham all but sacrificed his son Isaac; at the last minute he substituted a ram, caught by its horns in a thicket. That story echoed down through Jewish folklore as the event because of which God would save Israel, the people descended from Abraham.

This city is where King David, 'the man after God's own heart', set up his capital. This is where David's son Solomon built the temple where God was to be worshipped. This is the city which the Psalms sing about: beautiful Mount Zion, 'the joy of all the earth' (Psalm 48). This is the city the Babylonians destroyed. This is the city the Romans destroyed. This is the city where grief, and fresh hope, have lived as neighbours for three thousand years.

This city was where, according to the biblical prophets, the living God would reveal himself, to save not only Israel but the whole world. Back in Jesus' day, there were many who believed that this would happen very soon. And when you stand there, none of that is ancient history. The stones are full of it.

Put that whole story together, layer upon layer: the God of all the world acting in history to save all the world—and doing it in Jerusalem. And then take that multicoloured lens, and look through it at the scene which unfolds, not so very long ago—just the other day, really—as another young protester is casually liquidated by the occupying forces. It happens all the time. It's what occupying forces do to folk who think they're going to liberate their country and discover too late that there is an immovable object in the way of the irresistible force of their zeal, their longing for liberty. It's what happens to failed messiahs. It's what happened to Jesus.

Standing in the Church of the Holy Sepulchre, at the spot where Jesus of Nazareth

Remains of the walls that surrounded the old city of Jerusalem—'the joy of all the earth, Mount Zion... the city of the great King' *(Psalm 48:1)*.

was executed, I was in the middle of one of the greatest puzzles of history.

On the one hand, we know for certain that Jesus of Nazareth was crucified. That is one of the most secure facts in the history of the world. But on the other hand, we know that literally thousands of other Jews were crucified within fifty years either side of Jesus. There were two others crucified the very same day, right beside him.

What made Jesus special? Why do people all over the world tell the story of *his* death, rather than any of the others?

We know for certain that Jesus of Nazareth was crucified. That is one of the most secure facts in the history of the world. But on the other hand, we know that literally thousands of other Jews were crucified within fifty years either side of Jesus.

What made Jesus special? Why do people all over the world tell the story of his death, rather than any of the others?

An original vision

Supposing we could ask the rather motley crew who had been with Jesus up to that point why they had been following him. What would they have said?

They would have said that Jesus was different because of what he'd been doing and saying for the previous two or three years. Things have been happening, they would say, which drove us to believe that he was the one through whom our God, the God of all the world, would liberate us after all our suffering. He gave us fresh hope in the middle of our grief.

The Church of the Holy Sepulchre is thought by many to be built on the site of Jesus' crucifixion, burial and resurrection. The outcrop of rock believed to be Golgotha—'the place of a skull'—and the traditional catacomb of Joseph of Arimathea are both located within this extensive building.

We came here to Jerusalem with him because he was going to bring in the kingdom of God. We believed that our God would set us free at last—free from foreign oppression, free to live our lives as we always wanted to. We believed that our God would return at last, to live in this holy city. Jesus would be king; we would be his courtiers; and he would put Israel, and the whole world, to rights.

What was it that made Jesus' desperately disappointed followers conclude that his crucifixion was a victory, not a defeat? What was it made them say that this wasn't just a brutal and messy murder, but the decisive loving and saving act of the living God?

But of course, his execution put the lid on all that. Remember, it's failed messiahs who end up on crosses. This place saw the end of a beautiful dream.

So why did they go on regarding Jesus as special? With one voice they would reply: Because of what happened next. God raised him from the dead. We weren't expecting it, they would say; it wasn't part of our game-plan; but it happened. And gradually, bit by bit, we came to see that what happened here on that Friday afternoon was the drawing together of all those other Jerusalem-stories. This was how the kingdom was to come. This was how the prophecies would be fulfilled. This was what the temple was always pointing to. This was like Abraham sacrificing Isaac, only now it was the living God sacrificing his own beloved son. This was the place where the pain and the sin and the shame and the guilt of all the world, of all people, of all history before and since, was concentrated—and was dealt with once and for all. This was where the one true God acted to save and heal the whole world.

That's what Jesus' followers did find themselves driven to say. And to investigate that claim, it won't do simply to look at it from the outside. There is no such thing as neutrality or objectivity at this point. If you pin the history to the wall like a butterfly, you may be able to study it analytically, but you mustn't be surprised that it won't fly again. To get to the heart of it all, you have to live within the story and see what it does to you. That's what this book invites you to do.

We're going to look at the larger story that led up to the crucifixion. And we're going to look at the strange story that followed on from it. What was it, before and after, that made Jesus' desperately disappointed followers conclude that his crucifixion was a victory, not a defeat? What was it made them say that this wasn't just a brutal and messy murder, but the decisive loving and saving act of the living God?

And why on earth might we, in a different time and place, want to make that story our own?

The Lowest Point of History

In the fifteenth year of the reign of Emperor Tiberius, when Pontius Pilate was governor of Judea, and Herod was ruler of Galilee... the word of God came to John son of Zechariah in the wilderness. He went into all the region around the Jordan, proclaiming a baptism of repentance for the forgiveness of sins...

As the people were filled with expectation, and all were questioning in their hearts concerning John, whether he might be the Messiah, John answered all of them by saying, 'I baptize you with water; but one who is more powerful than I is coming; I am not worthy to untie the thong of his sandals. He will baptize you with the Holy Spirit and fire.

LUKE 3:1–3, 15–16

In those days Jesus came from Nazareth of Galilee and was baptized by John in the Jordan. And just as he was coming up out of the water, he saw the heavens torn apart and the Spirit descending like a dove on him. And a voice came from heaven, 'You are my Son, the Beloved; with you I am well pleased.'

And the Spirit immediately drove him out into the wilderness. He was in the wilderness forty days, tempted by Satan; and he was with the wild beasts; and the angels waited on him.

Now after John was arrested, Jesus came to Galilee, proclaiming the good news of God, and saying, 'The time is fulfilled, and the kingdom of God has come near; repent, and believe in the good news.'

MARK 1:9–15

The Jordan valley, just north of the Dead Sea, is the lowest point on the face of the earth: it's twelve hundred feet below sea level. If you want to get any lower than that, you'd have to dig.

What made John the Baptist want to come and spend his time out there? Well, if you were a Jew in the first century, the desert is where you would expect things to happen. In particular, it is where you would expect hope to be born again. But why there in particular?

To this day, Jews all around the world tell the story year by year of how their God rescued them out of slavery in Egypt—the great escape known as the Exodus. He brought them through the Red Sea. They spent forty years wandering in the wilderness until they arrived at the edge

After leading the Israelites out of Egypt, Moses brought them as far as these distant hills overlooking the Jordan valley. As then, the people of Jesus' day were looking for a new leader to save them from their enemies and show them the way ahead.

of the land God had promised them as home. Moses brought them that far, but then he died—up in the hills overlooking the valley. Joshua took over. And Joshua led the people across the Jordan river and into the Promised Land. They were home at last.

Because of all that, the Jordan wilderness became a vital symbol of new starts, new beginnings. The prophet Hosea saw Israel's God as a jilted lover; his bride, Israel, had left him and gone off with someone else. The marriage

covenant made between God and Israel under Moses had been broken. So he says, 'I will lead her into the wilderness, and woo her all over again' (Hosea 2:14). Then, after the people of Israel had been in exile in Babylon, the prophets spoke of getting ready a pathway in the wilderness—partly for Israel to come home to her land again, partly for Israel's God himself to come back. It's in the wilderness that God and Israel get it together again.

After Israel had been in exile in Babylon, the prophets spoke of getting ready a pathway in the wilderness—partly for Israel to come home again, partly for Israel's God himself to come back...

A voice cries out:
'In the wilderness prepare the way of the Lord,
make straight in the desert a highway for our God.
Every valley shall be lifted up,
and every mountain and hill be made low;
the uneven ground shall become level,
and the rough places a plain.
Then the glory of the Lord shall be revealed,
and all people shall see it together,
for the mouth of the Lord has spoken...
Get you up to a high mountain,
O Zion, herald of good tidings,
lift up your voice with strength,
O Jerusalem, herald of good tidings,
lift it up, do not fear,
say to the cities of Judah,
'Here is your God!'

ISAIAH 40:3–5, 9

In Jesus' day, Israel was in deep trouble. The people were living under the rule of the pagan Romans, with heavily compromised local politicians, and sliding deeper and deeper into debt. Not surprisingly, a number of groups arose, usually led by a would-be prophet or king. They weren't just after a change in the political leadership; they had a much bigger vision. They were hoping and praying that at last Israel's God himself would come and set the people free, bringing in the time of peace and justice. Usually such prophets and messiahs didn't live very long.

Just a few miles from the Jordan is the famous settlement at Qumran, where a religious group called Essenes lived. They were waiting

FACING PAGE:
Like some of the great prophets before him, Jesus retreated to the wilderness to escape from the crowds, clear his mind, listen for the voice of God, and prepare himself to take God's message back to the people.

The caves in which many of the Dead Sea Scrolls were found are situated just opposite the monastic settlement at Qumran (above). Hailed in 1948 as the greatest manuscript discovery of modern times, the Scrolls shed fascinating light on the part that one first-century sect believed it would play in establishing God's kingdom on earth.

for Israel's God to act, to defeat the Romans, to punish the people they saw as renegade Jews, up the hill in Jerusalem, and to establish his kingdom of justice and peace. Then, when the Romans closed in on them, they hid their precious writings in the caves nearby. We call these writings the Dead Sea Scrolls.

Yet another group clustered around a man called John. He's the only one of the bunch who has had an opera written about him, but that's not what makes him special. He was doing something the others weren't. He was plunging people into the Jordan. The Greek word for 'plunge' or 'dip', or 'splash' or even 'flood' or 'drown' is *baptizo*, so they called John's plunging 'baptism', and they called John himself 'John the Plunger', or, with the Greek word, 'John the Baptizer'.

In Jesus' day, Israel was in deep trouble. The people were living under the rule of the pagan Romans, with heavily compromised local politicians, and sliding deeper and deeper into debt. Not surprisingly, a number of groups arose, usually led by a would-be prophet or king.... Usually such prophets and messiahs didn't live very long.

It wasn't, of course, that John thought people needed a wash, though the symbolism of cleansing may have been present as well. John was symbolically re-enacting what happened when the children of Israel came through the River Jordan and into the promised land. This is an Exodus-symbol. It is all about salvation, rescue, liberty, the new start that the people had longed for. Israel would come home at last; God would come home too; evil would be defeated, and the true God would become the king of all the earth.

Strong stuff, especially if you happened to be on the wrong side. John didn't mince his words. The world is full of injustice: if there is a God, he must care about that; if he cares, he must do something about it; and since this was the lowest point of history as far as Israel was concerned, he must do something *right here and right now*.

There wouldn't have been much argument about all this: the Jews of the time were being heavily taxed, driven off their land, furious about pagans polluting their culture. They wanted God's kingdom all right, and they wanted it soon. John was saying this day after day. People were flocking here from all over to be plunged into the river as a sign that they wanted to be part of the renewed people of God, the people who would be rescued from exile at last.

After Joshua led the Israelites across the Jordan to the Promised Land, this river became a symbol of salvation and hope for the Jewish people. John the Baptist called the people here to prepare for the coming of Jesus, 'the Lamb of God who takes away the sins of the world' *(John 1:29)*.

A new leader

Among the crowds there came a man a year or so younger than John: his cousin from up north. His name was the same as that of the leader who had taken over from Moses all those years ago: Jeshua, Joshua, or in Greek *Jesous*, Jesus. And, like Moses handing on the torch to Joshua, John pointed to Jesus as the one who would take the movement forward from there.

Jesus joined in with John's movement, and bided his time. Then, when the authorities came for John, as they were bound to do sooner or later, Jesus took a deep breath and began his own independent movement. Now is the time, he said; the days of preparation are over. This is the moment when our God is at last becoming king.

Jesus joined in with John's movement, and bided his time. Then, when the authorities came for John, as they were bound to do sooner or later, Jesus took a deep breath and began his own independent movement.

Jesus went through Galilee, village by village, telling people that the kingdom of God was happening now. Now, at last, Israel's oppression would be over. God would come home to save the people. Now, at last, with the world at its lowest point, evil would be defeated and justice would triumph. No wonder they followed him. No wonder they hung on his words. He was telling them the story they wanted to hear, the story of justice and hope at last.

But what was original about Jesus' version of this message?

Well, as he told the story, he was also adjusting it in a number of ways. Justice and peace wouldn't come, as many had supposed,

Jesus believed that in the end he, himself, would go down, alone, to the lowest point of human experience. Somehow, strangely, through that act God would defeat evil.

through military revolt against Rome. They wouldn't come through Israel simply having every aspiration endorsed and underwritten. Like the prophets of old, and like John the Baptizer himself, Jesus warned his contemporaries that when the kingdom of God arrived it would be a doubly revolutionary event. Yes, it would overturn all the power structures of the world; but it would also overturn all the expectations about how that would happen.

So how, then, would it happen? Well, Jesus believed that in the end he, himself, would go down, alone, to the lowest point of human experience. Somehow, strangely, through that act God would defeat evil; justice and peace would be born again; and the whole world would be brought home at last.

FACING PAGE
Nazareth, the town in which Jesus grew up. The Gospel of Luke records that after Jesus had been baptized by John he returned to Galilee and began to teach in the synagogues. But when he came to Nazareth, so incensed were the people by what he said that they 'drove him out of the town, and led him up to the brow of the hill on which their town was built, so that they might hurl him off the cliff' *(Luke 4:29)*.

3

The Two-Edged Story

Now all the tax collectors and sinners were coming near to listen to him. And the Pharisees and the scribes were grumbling and saying, 'This fellow welcomes sinners and eats with them.' …

Then Jesus said, 'There was a man who had two sons. The younger of them said to his father, "Father, give me the share of the property that will belong to me." So he divided his property between them. A few days later the younger son gathered all he had and travelled to a distant country, and there he squandered his property in dissolute living. When he had spent everything, a severe famine took place throughout that country, and he began to be in need. So he went and hired himself out to one of the citizens of that country, who sent him to his fields to feed the pigs. He would gladly have filled himself with the pods that the pigs were eating; and no one gave him anything. But when he came to himself he said, "How many of my father's hired hands have bread enough and to spare, but here I am dying of hunger! I will get up and go to my father, and I will say to him, 'Father, I have sinned against heaven and before you; I am no longer worthy to be called your son; treat me like one of your hired hands.'"

'So he set off and went to his father. But while he was still far off, his father saw him and was filled with compassion; he ran and put his arms around him and kissed him. Then the son said to him, "Father, I have sinned against heaven and before you; I am no longer worthy to be called your son." But the father said to his slaves, "Quickly, bring out a robe—the best one—and put it on him; put a ring on his finger and sandals on his feet. And get the fatted calf and kill it, and let us eat and celebrate; for this son of mine was dead and is alive again; he was lost and is found!" And they began to celebrate.

'Now his elder son was in the field; and when he came and approached the house, he heard music and dancing. He called one of the slaves and asked what was going on. He replied, "Your brother has come, and your father has killed the fatted calf, because he has got him back safe and sound." Then he became angry and refused to go in. His father came out and began to plead with him. But he answered his

father, "Listen! For all these years I have been working like a slave for you, and I have never disobeyed your command; yet you have never given me even a young goat so that I might celebrate with my friends. But when this son of yours came back, who has devoured your property with prostitutes, you killed the fatted calf for him!" Then the father said to him, "Son, you are always with me, and all that is mine is yours. But we had to celebrate and rejoice, because this brother of yours was dead and has come to life; he was lost and has been found."'

LUKE 15:1–2, 11–32

In our modern culture, we sometimes imagine that stories are kids' stuff: little illustrations, while abstract ideas are the real thing.

So Jesus' stories, people say, were just 'earthly stories with heavenly meaning'. But that's rubbish! Stories are far more powerful than that. Stories create worlds. Tell the story differently, and you change the world. And that's what Jesus aimed to do.

People in Jesus' world *knew* that stories meant business; that stories were a way of getting to grips with reality. But understanding the reality of Jesus' stories today isn't always easy. People in his day would have known what he was talking about;

Jesus' stories, people say, were just 'earthly stories with heavenly meaning'. But that's rubbish! Stories are far more powerful than that. Stories create worlds. Tell the story differently, and you change the world. And that's what Jesus aimed to do.

but for us, it's a matter of making the historical effort to get back inside the minds of the original audience...

A revolutionary message

In the homes and villages of first-century Palestine, everybody knew who was who. In particular, everybody knew who the senior people were. This society put a high value on age and wisdom. They respected their elders; and the elders had, and acted with, great dignity.

If you're an elder, with all this dignity, there's one thing you don't do. You never, ever run. We have got used to seeing Presidents of

In biblical times, the elders of a community were accorded great respect for their years of accumulated wisdom and experience.

The most striking prophetic picture of the return from exile had been Ezekiel's vision of the valley of dry bones...

The hand of the Lord came upon me, and he brought me out by the spirit of the Lord and set me down in the middle of a valley; it was full of bones. He led me all around them; there were very many lying in the valley, and they were very dry. He said to me, 'Mortal, can these bones live?' I answered, 'O Lord God, you know.' Then he said to me, 'Prophesy to these bones, and say to them: O dry bones, hear the word of the Lord. Thus says the Lord God to these bones: I will cause breath to enter you, and you shall live. I will lay sinews on you, and will cause flesh to come upon you, and cover you with skin, and put breath in you, and you shall live; and you shall know that I am the Lord.'...

Then he said to me, 'Mortal, these bones are the whole house of Israel. They say, "Our bones are dried up, and our hope is lost; we are cut off completely." Therefore prophesy, and say to them, Thus says the Lord God: I am going to open your graves, and bring you up from your graves, O my people; and I will bring you back to the land of Israel. And you shall know that I am the Lord, when I open your graves, and bring you up from your graves, O my people. I will put my spirit within you, and you shall live, and I will place you on your own soil; then you shall know that I, the Lord, have spoken and will act, says the Lord.'

EZEKIEL 37:1–6, 11–14

the United States on TV, going for a morning jog. That would have been unthinkable in the society Jesus lived in. Even to walk a bit too briskly would have been to lose your dignity.

But Jesus told a story about a senior, respected figure who threw his dignity out of the window and ran down the street. The shock, in his culture, would be like the Prime Minister appearing for a Press conference in a bathing costume.

The story is well known, but usually we don't appreciate it. Let's take it from the beginning. It could be called the story of the Running Father, but it's more familiarly known as the story of the Prodigal Son.

There was a man who had two sons. The younger one asked his father for his share of the inheritance. He wanted it right away. Now, that would be totally shocking to the people who first heard it. In our society, sons often ask fathers for cash down in advance. But in this sort of village, such a request is like saying 'I wish you were dead.' It puts a curse on the father.

And the father actually agrees to the request. He says, in effect, 'OK, you want me out of the way: be my guest; here's the property.' The young son sells off his share of the land—that must have been pretty galling to the father, too—and makes off for foreign parts. The next bit is obvious. He spends the cash; he runs out of luck; he ends up feeding pigs—about as low as a Jewish boy could sink. But something in the far recesses of his mind tells him that it might be worth going back home.

That's the next shock. In that culture, someone in disgrace doesn't go home. He's put a curse on his father; he has brought shame on the whole family. But home he goes, anyway; and then the miracle occurs. Here is the old man, his father, *running down the road to meet him*. Not only that; he throws a party for the whole village. 'This my son was dead, and is alive again.'

Not surprisingly, those who maintain the traditional values are shocked. The older brother, in particular, is furious; so much so that he, too, shames his father, by complaining at him in front of all their guests. Even in our society, we'd find a son being rude to his father in public a bit hard to take. But, instead of telling off the elder son, the father gently reasons with him. He wants him to understand the apparently disgraceful thing he, the father, has just done. Again, the father abandons his dignity. 'This your brother was dead, and is alive again; he was lost, and is found.'

The last shock in the story is that it ends a few lines too soon. As if it were a movie that freezes the last frame just when you wanted to know what happened next, Jesus leaves the story hanging in the air. In that culture particularly, his hearers would want to know: what happened next? Did the older brother relent, and come back in? How did they all get on after that? But the listeners—like us—are expected to work it out for themselves.

What's he getting at?

So what *is* it all about? What is the reality behind it? It's so often been turned into a general story about God's love for us, his prodigal children. And at one level that's right.

But, if you were a first-century Jewish audience, there'd be more to it than that. You'd be longing to hear a story like this. A story about a scapegrace young son who goes off in disgrace into foreign parts, and is then given an astonishing welcome back home—why, this is the story of Israel going into exile, and then at last coming back again! This is the story about the kingdom of God, about Israel's liberation, that they wanted to hear.

But why does Jesus tell it this way, with these characters? At the heart of the story is *the reason for the party*. Jesus was being heavily criticized by the guardians of the ancestral traditions because he was celebrating the kingdom, not with the righteous and the religious elite, but with all and sundry—with the riff-raff, the no-goods, the down-and-outs. And, in the process, he wasn't just throwing his own dignity to the winds; he was threatening God's dignity, and, with it, the hope of the whole nation.

Jesus was being heavily criticized by the guardians of the ancestral traditions because he was celebrating the kingdom, not with the righteous and the religious elite, but with all and sundry—with the riff-raff, the no-goods, the down-and-outs.

Yes, says Jesus: Just like a father who... The story explains why Jesus has been acting in the shameless way he has. He is bringing in the kingdom of God; he is bringing about the real homecoming, the real return from exile; so of course there has to be a party. Of course you have to celebrate.

Who cares about dignity when the kingdom of God is arriving? The most striking prophetic picture of the return from exile had been Ezekiel's vision of the valley of dry bones, all coming to life: when Israel is restored after exile, it will be like the resurrection of the dead.

Yes, says Jesus: this my son, this your brother, was dead and is alive again—Israel is alive again. This is the restoration you have been waiting for.

Jesus told all sorts of stories. Each one was like a stick of dynamite, ready to explode at any moment. He went to and fro, planting these explosive charges in people's hearts and minds. The kingdom of God, God's new rule, was going to change everything.

So what about the elder brother in the story? The elder brother stands for the people who don't want Jesus' version of the kingdom-story. They want to keep their own version intact. They want to hang on to their personal or national or cultural dignity, rather than go chasing after this strange prophet who is celebrating the kingdom with all the wrong people. So Jesus lines them up with the people who didn't want Israel to return from exile. In the Jewish Bible, that means the Samaritans. And the story points to the question: what's going to happen next? Jesus wants them all, including the grumblers, to join in the party. But will they?

Jesus told all sorts of stories of this kind. Each one was like a stick of dynamite, ready to explode at any moment. He went to and fro, planting these explosive charges in people's hearts and minds. The kingdom of God, God's new rule, was going to change everything; the whole world would be turned upside down. Very undignified that would be. So who was prepared to live by these stories? Who was ready to throw caution to the winds and join in this new world?

That's the question that echoes down through history from that day to this.

4

Message from the Mountain

Jesus went throughout Galilee, teaching in their synagogues and proclaiming the good news of the kingdom and curing every disease and every sickness among the people... And great crowds followed him from Galilee, the Decapolis, Jerusalem, Judea, and from beyond the Jordan.

When Jesus saw the crowds, he went up the mountain; and after he sat down, his disciples came to him. Then he began to speak, and taught them, saying:

'Blessed are the poor in spirit, for theirs is the kingdom of heaven.

'Blessed are those who mourn, for they will be comforted.

'Blessed are the meek, for they will inherit the earth.

'Blessed are those who hunger and thirst for righteousness, for they will be filled.

'Blessed are the merciful, for they will receive mercy.

'Blessed are the pure in heart, for they will see God.

'Blessed are the peacemakers, for they will be called children of God.

'Blessed are those who are persecuted for righteousness' sake, for theirs is the kingdom of heaven.

'Blessed are you when people revile you and persecute you and utter all kinds of evil against you falsely on my account. Rejoice and be glad, for your reward is great in heaven, for in the same way they persecuted the prophets who were before you.

'You are the salt of the earth; but if salt has lost its taste, how can its saltiness be restored? It is no longer good for anything, but is thrown out and trampled under foot.

'You are the light of the world. A city built on a hill cannot be hid. No one after lighting a lamp puts it under the bushel basket, but on the lampstand, and it gives light to all in the house. In the same way, let your light shine before others, so that they may see your good works and give glory to your Father in heaven...

'You have heard that it was said, "An eye for an eye and a tooth for a tooth." But I say to you, Do not resist an evildoer. But if anyone strikes you on the right cheek, turn the other also; and if anyone wants to sue you and take your coat, give your cloak as well; and if anyone forces you to go one mile, go also the second mile. Give to everyone who begs from you, and do not refuse anyone who wants to borrow from you.

'You have heard that it was said, "You shall love your neighbour and hate your enemy." But I say to you, Love your enemies and pray for those who persecute you, so that you may be children of your Father in heaven; for he makes his sun rise on the evil and on the good, and sends rain on the righteous and on the unrighteous.'

MATTHEW 4:23, 25; 5:1–16, 38–45

In the time of Jesus, the hills above the Sea of Galilee used to be the hang-out for holy revolutionaries, for outlaws ready to defeat the pagan Romans and to bring in the kingdom of God—by force if necessary. Up in the hills there are caves; a generation before Jesus, some of the revolutionaries had been smoked out from them by King Herod.

Nearby is the so-called 'Mount of Beatitudes', the traditional site where Jesus preached his most famous sermon.

But why did Jesus go up there to instruct his followers? And, for that matter, why did they all follow him up into the hills? What was it about his message that made them down tools and set off after him?

A good many people think that the Sermon on the Mount is the centre of Christianity. But what's it all about?

To hear some people talk, and from the look of the 'Mount of Beatitudes' today, you'd think that the Sermon on the Mount consisted simply of Jesus telling people to be nice to each other. Now there's a bit of that, of course; but you don't go all the way up a mountain just to learn

Some of the caves in these Galilean hills became a refuge for Jewish outlaws and revolutionaries, intent on resisting the Roman occupation of their land.

At the end of his great Sermon on the Mount, Jesus offered a solemn challenge to all that the temple stood for...

'Everyone then who hears these words of mine and acts on them will be like a wise man who built his house on rock. The rain fell, the floods came, and the winds blew and beat on that house, but it did not fall, because it had been founded on rock. And everyone who hears these words of mine and does not act on them will be like a foolish man who built his house on sand. The rain fell, and the floods came, and the winds blew and beat against that house, and it fell—and great was its fall!'

Now when Jesus had finished saying these things, the crowds were astounded at his teaching, for he taught them as one having authority, and not as their scribes.

MATTHEW 7:24–29

that. The popular image of the sermon is of a gentle, quietly romantic view of the religious life, somewhat detached from the world.

To hear others talk, you'd think the only thing Jesus was talking about was how to go to heaven when they died. Actually, there's almost nothing about that in the whole sermon.

A manifesto for change

So what *is* it all about? Well, when Jesus first gave what we now call the Sermon on the Mount, he was staging something that would look to us much more like a political rally. He was like someone drumming up support for a new movement, a new great cause. He was calling his hearers, quite simply, to a new way of being Israel, a new way of being God's people for the world.

To get to grips with what *that* means we need to step back into Israel's oldest traditions. Why was there a 'chosen people' in the first place? Well, according to the Bible, the creator-God chose Abraham and his family, the ancestors of Israel, as his means of addressing, and solving, the problem of the whole world. Israel was called to be a people with a purpose: the people through whom God would eventually put the world to rights. Israel was called to be the light of the world, the salt of the earth. They were proud of their city, Jerusalem, set on a hill in Judea.

When Jesus first gave what we now call the Sermon on the Mount, he was staging something that would look to us much more like a political rally. He was like someone drumming up support for a new movement, a new great cause.

Jesus is saying: follow me, and we can make it happen! Follow me, and you *will* be the light of the world, the salt of the earth. The city set on the hill can't be hidden: it's supposed to be there for the benefit of the whole world.

From his point of view, Israel at that time was making a pretty poor fist of being the light of the world. Many of Jesus' contemporaries were hot-headed, zealous would-be revolutionaries. Was that the way the kingdom would come? Was that how to be the light of the world?

Jesus' answer was an unequivocal No. He was calling and challenging his contemporaries

Jesus encouraged his disciples to see themselves as 'the light of the world', comparing them to a city on a hill that cannot be hidden. In Old Testament times the prophet Isaiah had spoken of Israel's calling to be 'a light to the nations, to open the eyes that are blind' *(Isaiah 42:7)*.

to be the people of God in a radically new way. He solemnly announced God's blessings—but he blessed all the wrong people: the poor, the mourners, the meek, the hungry, the merciful, the pure in heart, the persecuted, the peacemakers. When the real revolution comes, he seems to be saying, the revolutionaries won't get a look in.

Maybe his mother had taught him her song: God has filled the hungry with good things, but the rich he has sent empty away (Luke 1:53). This is a dangerous message, an exciting, deeply subversive challenge.

Turning the world inside out

Jesus was turning everything inside out—or rather, you might say, turning it all outside in. He was insisting that outward obedience wasn't enough. God wanted a revolution of everything—including people's hearts.

Some people have read all that stuff about turning the other cheek as though it's an invitation to 'be a doormat for Jesus'. It isn't. When Jesus says 'Don't resist evil', this translates the Greek word *antistenai*, which refers to the resistance movement. If someone hits you on your right cheek, they will have done it with the back of the hand—as though you were beneath their contempt. Offer them the other cheek, says Jesus: then, if they hit you again, they will have to admit that you are a fellow human being, an equal—someone who is entitled to respect.

Jesus was calling and challenging his contemporaries to be the people of God in a radically new way. He solemnly announced God's blessings—but he blessed all the wrong people: the poor, the mourners, the meek, the hungry, the merciful, the pure in heart, the persecuted, the peacemakers.

The whole sermon is about taking the great risk of faith: that to change the world, right now, you need to believe that God is God, and to let that turn your national and personal priorities upside down. Like somebody learning how to dive, Jesus' hearers have to learn to let go, to throw themselves off their safe perch and trust themselves to the water. Can you imagine what people would say to a politician who made that the central plank of his campaign speech today?

So Jesus rounds off the sermon with a warning. Don't suppose that this is just one option among many. This is the *only* way to go. This is the only true-Israel way, the only way forward for God's people. This is what the law and the prophets were all about. But look out. All sorts of other people are offering all sorts of other agendas; they will speak sweetly, they will tell you all the things you want to hear, but at the end of the day there'll be nothing to show for it (Matthew 7:15–20).

The real revolutionaries

Some of his hearers did follow him; and,
from those who did, he called twelve in particular,
and brought them up into the hills again,
to commission them for special work
(Mark 3:13–19).

When Jesus took his twelve disciples and gave them their marching orders, it would have looked like the founding of a revolutionary movement. But this was a revolution with a difference....

Now we mustn't think of that as some kind of religious ceremony, a kind of primitive ordination service. Remember who normally hid out in those hills. So when Jesus took his twelve disciples up there and gave them their marching orders, it would have looked a lot more like the founding of a revolutionary movement. But this was a revolution with a difference. Jesus' people were to be the real light of the world.

This message echoes down from the hills of Galilee to the gates of the holy city, Jerusalem itself, seventy miles to the south. The focal point of Jerusalem was the temple, the house of God, often referred to simply as 'the house'; it

'On the holy mount stands the city he founded; the Lord loves the gates of Zion.' *(Psalm 87:1)*

The seven-branched candlestick, the *menorah*, one of the most sacred objects to be housed in the temple, was carried away by the Romans after the sacking of Jerusalem in AD 70.

was built on the rock of Mount Zion, and the Jews looked to it as the great symbol of their security.

At the end of his great Sermon on the Mount, Jesus offered a solemn challenge to all that the temple stood for.

Anyone, he says, who hears my words and does them—that will be the really wise person, the one who built his house on the rock. *This*, in other words, is the true temple-movement. God is doing, in Jesus, the real thing to which the temple had been pointing all along. This is religious and political dynamite! And along with the challenge goes the solemn warning: unless you follow the way I am offering you, you will be like a foolish person, building your house on the sand. Winds and storms will come and beat on that house, and it will fall with a great crash.

Well, the winds came, the storms blew, and the crash happened. The leaders of Israel in

Jesus' day refused his challenge, didn't listen to his warning, and continued to pursue their dream of military revolution, keeping the light for themselves in order to ensure that they were the only light in the world. Many of the ordinary Jews followed their leaders into ruin. And the house of God, the temple, was destroyed by the Romans, just forty years after Jesus had warned them about it.

Jesus' challenge and warning echo down the centuries, and out across the whole world. Build your house on the rock; that's the only way to go. There is a way to be truly human; it's the opposite of what most people think is the right way, but it's the only way that will work. Anything else is like building on sand.

If we wanted to take this seriously, it would mean taking a hard, fresh look at God's call to serve him in the world: the call to work out God's care for creation, and to implement God's justice, especially for those in great need. Again and again human beings use this vocation as an excuse for exploiting the world and oppressing each other. If we build our house on sand like that, it will fall with a great crash.

But if we really had the courage to build the house on the good news of Jesus, it would become the light of the world. As Jesus might have said, Is there anyone out there listening?

5

The Centre of the Cosmos

Then they came to Jerusalem. And he entered the temple and began to drive out those who were selling and those who were buying in the temple, and he overturned the tables of the money-changers and the seats of those who sold doves; and he would not allow anyone to carry anything through the temple. He was teaching and saying, 'Is it not written,

> *"My house shall be called a house of prayer for all the nations"?*
> *But you have made it a den of robbers.'*

And when the chief priests and the scribes heard it, they kept looking for a way to kill him; for they were afraid of him, because the whole crowd was spellbound by his teaching.

MARK 11:15–18

When I first came to Jerusalem, I tried several times to get in to the Temple Mount, and each time I failed.

Once I got caught in the rush as thousands of worshippers were leaving after their time of prayer. Another time the whole area was sealed off after some violent confrontations between rival groups. And so on.

Not surprising, really. This, after all, is the place where, in biblical tradition, the living God chose to meet with his people. This is where Solomon built the first temple. This is where the greatest triumphs and the greatest tragedies of the Jewish people have been concentrated. There, too, the prophet Mohammad is said to have ascended to heaven. After two Jewish temples had stood there, and one or two pagan ones, the Muslims built the Dome of the Rock and the al-Aqsa Mosque, which you can still see today.

The Jewish temple that existed back then wasn't simply a large building in one part of the city.

This plan of first-century Jerusalem shows what a dominant position was held by the temple and its courtyards in relation to the rest of the city.

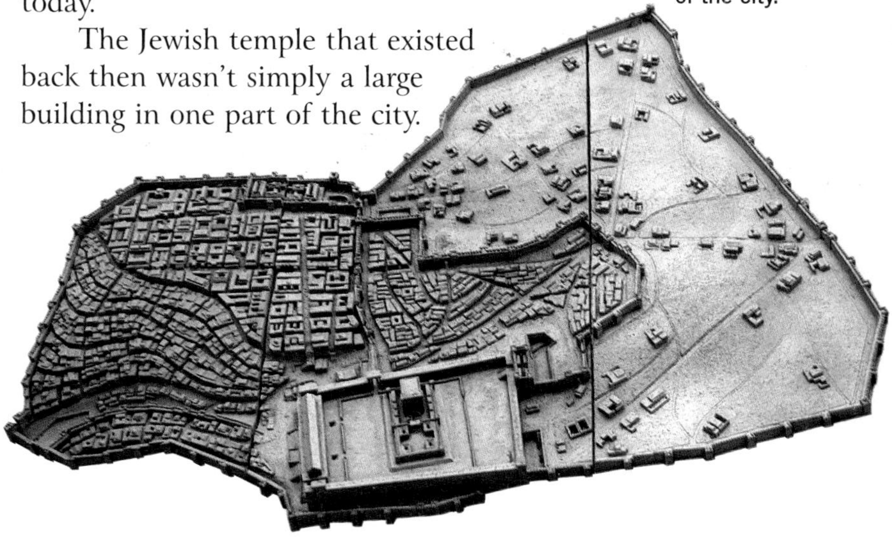

It's more that Jerusalem was a temple with a city around it!

But the temple wasn't just at the centre of the city. It was also at the centre of Jewish worship. They believed it was the centre of the cosmos itself.

Back when this second Jewish temple was standing, a young Jewish prophet rode in on a donkey and turned the place upside down.

Why did he do it? Was it simply an act of protest or, like so many of Jesus' actions, was there more to it than that?

To answer that question we have to go to the other end of the country, a hundred miles

It was at Caesarea Philippi, near the slopes of Mount Hermon, that Jesus received the recognition from his disciples that he was the Christ, the Messiah, marking a turning-point that was to lead to his return to Jerusalem, and to death at the hands of the Romans.

north, to the place the Romans called Caesarea Philippi, where there was an old shrine of the god Pan. It's on the slopes of Mount Hermon, which is tall enough, even in the heat of summer, to have snow on the top all year.

The turning point

Jesus brought his twelve followers to Caesarea Philippi, and asked them how they rated his career so far, and where they thought it was going (Mark 8:27—9:1). 'Oh,' they said 'lots of people think you're a prophet.' 'But you,' he said, 'Who do you say I am?'

Peter spoke for them all. 'You're the king,' he said. 'You are God's anointed one. You're the one we've been waiting for—the one God has chosen to set us free.'

From that moment on, the Galilean movement around Jesus had a new focus. Kings have to go to Jerusalem if they are to be crowned. And, in particular, kings have to cleanse or rebuild the temple. In ancient Britain, King Arthur had to pull the sword out of the stone to show he was the true king. In ancient Judaism, when the king came he would cleanse the temple. He might even have to destroy it and rebuild it. That's what some of Israel's greatest kings had done in the past. Some people, even, with no right to kingship had done it, to stake their claim.

So they set off for Jerusalem. Jesus' followers, pretty clearly, thought Jesus was going to be the ordinary sort of revolutionary king. They even began to argue about who would get which jobs in his council of state. Jesus kept telling them it wasn't going to be quite like that; but they didn't listen (Mark 9:33–37; 10:35–45).

What was Jesus' revolution all about? At its heart, he was remaking the people of God around himself, and telling everybody that they were freely welcome in it.

So what was *Jesus'* revolution all about? At its heart, he was remaking the people of God around himself, and telling everybody that they were freely welcome in it. So it wasn't only when he got to Jerusalem that he and the temple were clashing. All through his work, he was offering people the sort of blessing you could only get at the temple itself. He was offering them nothing less than the forgiveness of their sins—right there and then.

A new authority

In Jericho, on the way from Galilee to Jerusalem, he went to lunch with a notoriously crooked tax collector, and then had the effrontery to announce that the man was forgiven and restored as a full member of the community, a proper child of Abraham (Luke 19:1–10). Zacchaeus didn't have to go to Jerusalem, to the temple, to be forgiven and restored. Jesus did it for him right there.

Within that system, such actions were highly provocative. It was like someone today offering a convicted criminal a free pardon, and doing it on his own authority. It challenged everything that the temple in Jerusalem stood for. He was claiming to do and be exactly what the temple was and did.

So when Jesus finally came to Jerusalem, the place quite simply wasn't big enough for both of them—for him and the temple. The temple, in any case, was widely regarded as corrupt and in need of reform; and who better to challenge it than a prophet from Galilee, announcing the kingdom of God? So he came into the temple. The place was packed with pilgrims; and he totally disrupted the system. He overturned the money-changers' tables. He drove away the people selling animals for sacrifice. For a short while, in a powerful and symbolic fashion, he stopped the whole place from functioning. He prevented the temple doing what it was there to do.

Jesus' action wasn't designed as a take-over bid. It was much deeper and more powerful than that. It was an acted parable, a symbol of judgment. It was like someone burning a flag, or tearing up a contract. It was saying: this place has forfeited the right to be the home of the living God. It is under judgment. It's ready to be pulled down.

But what would replace it?

'Happy are those whom you choose and bring near to live in your courts. We shall be satisfied with the goodness of your house, your holy temple.' *(Psalm 65:4)*

A few days later, Jesus acted out another symbol, which many have seen as his answer to this question. He got his twelve disciples together, and they celebrated the freedom-meal, the Passover, the meal that commemorated the Jews' escape from Egypt many centuries earlier.

But, again, Jesus turned the symbolism of the meal in a new direction. The real Passover, the real act of liberation, was about to happen. And he would be at the centre of it. All that the temple had stood for would now be summed up in the cross, the last great symbolic event of Jesus' life.

Jesus believed that this new kingdom, this new rule of God, would come through something he had to do himself, alone. He had to go to the very eye of the storm, to the place where evil was doing its worst, and offer himself, his own life, as the means of defeating that evil at last.

You see, Jesus believed that this new kingdom, this new rule of God, would come, but not by simply rebuilding the temple in a bricks-and-mortar sense; nor by leading a military revolution to drive out the pagan Romans and establishing a free Jewish state. It was going to come through something he had to do himself, alone. He had to go to the very eye of the storm, to the place where evil was doing its worst, and offer himself, his own life, as the means of defeating that evil at last. He would exhaust that evil in himself. He had to embody, in himself, all that Passover, the freedom-celebration, had pointed towards.

Jesus believed that Israel's whole destiny, to be the people of God for the world, to be God's way of saving the world, was reaching its climax; and that his life, and ultimately his death, were to be the means of bringing that about.

As the ancient prophets had foretold, Israel and the world would finally be liberated, the kingdom of God would finally come, when the Servant of the Lord went to his death, bearing in his own body the weight of the world's evil...

He was despised and rejected by others;
a man of suffering and acquainted with infirmity;
and as one from whom others hide their faces
he was despised, and we held him of no account.

Surely he has borne our infirmities
and carried our diseases;
yet we accounted him stricken,
struck down by God, and afflicted.
But he was wounded for our transgressions,
crushed for our iniquities;
upon him was the punishment that made us whole,
and by his bruises we are healed.
All we like sheep have gone astray;
we have all turned to our own way,
and the Lord has laid on him
the iniquity of us all.

He was oppressed, and he was afflicted,
yet he did not open his mouth;
like a lamb that is led to the slaughter,
and like a sheep that before its shearers is silent,
so he did not open his mouth.
By a perversion of justice he was taken away.
Who could have imagined his future?
For he was cut off from the land of the living,
stricken for the transgression of my people.
They made his grave with the wicked
and his tomb with the rich,
although he had done no violence,
and there was no deceit in his mouth.

ISAIAH 53:3–9

As the ancient prophets had foretold, Israel and the world would finally be liberated, the kingdom of God would finally come, when the Servant of the Lord went to his death, bearing in his own body the weight of the world's evil.

What the temple stood for—the saving presence of Israel's God at the very centre of the world—would be summed up in the violent death, at the hands of the pagans, of the young Jew who carried on his shoulders the pain and grief of the whole world. This was how sins would be forgiven. This was how the real Exodus would happen. This would be how the shameless, reckless love of the creator-God would come running down the road to embrace the whole world.

When we reflect on that young Jew, and the strange things he did, and the strange fate he met—what does it do to us? Was he just mad, living on a dream that made him out of touch with reality?

Or supposing there was something to the old Jewish belief that this place really was the centre of the cosmos. Could it be that Jesus had tapped into the secret of what the world is really all about? Could it be that he really did take hold of the small rudder by which the mighty ship of world history can be turned, and manage to swing it in the right direction, even though it cost him his life?

6

Back to the Garden

When they came to the place that is called The Skull, they crucified Jesus there with the criminals, one on his right and one on his left. [Then Jesus said, 'Father, forgive them; for they do not know what they are doing.'] And they cast lots to divide his clothing. And the people stood by, watching; but the leaders scoffed at him, saying, 'He saved others; let him save himself if he is the Messiah of God, his chosen one!' The soldiers also mocked him, coming up and offering him sour wine, and saying, 'If you are the King of the Jews, save yourself!' There was also an inscription over him, 'This is the King of the Jews'...

It was now about noon, and darkness came over the whole land until three in the afternoon, while the sun's light failed; and the curtain of the temple was torn in two. Then Jesus, crying with a loud voice, said, 'Father, into your hands I commend my spirit.' Having said this, he breathed his last. When the centurion saw what had taken place, he praised God and said, 'Certainly this man was innocent.' And when all the crowds who had gathered there for this spectacle saw what had taken place, they returned home, beating their breasts. But all his acquaintances, including the women who had followed him from Galilee, stood at a distance, watching these things.

Now there was a good and righteous man named Joseph, who, though a member of the council, had not agreed to their plan and action. He came from the Jewish town of Arimathea, and he was waiting expectantly for the kingdom of God. This man went to Pilate and asked for the body of Jesus. Then he took it down, wrapped it in a linen cloth, and laid it in a rock-hewn tomb where no one had ever been laid. It was the day of Preparation, and the sabbath was beginning. The women who had come with him from Galilee followed, and they saw the tomb and how his body was laid. Then they returned, and prepared spices and ointments.

On the sabbath they rested according to the commandment.

But on the first day of the week, at early dawn, they came to the tomb, taking the spices that they had prepared. They found the stone rolled away from the tomb, but when they went in, they did not find the body. While they were perplexed about this, suddenly two men in dazzling clothes stood beside them. The women were terrified and bowed their faces to the ground, but the men said to them, 'Why do you look for the living among the dead? He is not here, but has risen. Remember how he told you, while he was still in Galilee, that the Son of Man must be handed over to sinners, and be crucified, and on the third day rise again.' Then they remembered his words, and returning from the tomb, they told all this to the eleven and to all the rest. Now it was Mary Magdalene, Joanna, Mary the mother of James, and the other women with them who told this to the apostles. But these words seemed to them an idle tale, and they did not believe them. But Peter got up and ran to the tomb; stooping and looking in, he saw the linen cloths by themselves; then he went home, amazed at what had happened.

LUKE 23:33–38, 44–56; 24:1–12

The oddest thing about Christianity is why it got going at all.

We know of ten or a dozen other movements that arose in Palestine within about a hundred years either side of Jesus. There seem to have been lots of other young Jews who were prepared to risk all at the head of a little revolutionary group, in the hope that their God would act through them and bring in his kingdom.

One of the best known was a man called Judas the Galilean, who led an uprising around the time of Jesus' birth. He and hundreds of others were picked up by the authorities, and they were crucified (Josephus, *Antiquities*, 17:271–98; *War*, 2:56–79).

Almost exactly a hundred years after Jesus' death, there was another great revolution, led by Simeon ben-Kosiba. Some of the leading Jewish teachers said 'Here at last is the Messiah!' He, too, like all the rest, was hunted down by the authorities, and killed.

In each case, the death of the leader meant the end of the movement. The exception proves the rule: Judas the Galilean seems to have had a family, to whom his disappointed followers turned. One of the would-be messiahs during the Jewish War of 66–70 was a man called Menahem, the leader of the Sicarii, the dagger-

Masada, the rock-fortress on which Jewish rebels made their last stand from AD70 to 73. When eventually the Romans managed to scale the rock and break through the walls, they were met with a deathly silence: the defenders had killed themselves and their families, rather than surrender.

men. He was the grandson of Judas the Galilean. When he was killed by a rival group of Jews, a relative called Eleazar took up the leadership. The group ended its days on Masada, finally committing mass suicide when the Romans closed in.

The rule, then, seems clear. If you follow a messiah and he gets killed, you obviously backed the wrong horse. You should either give up, or get yourself another leader from the same family.

So why did the followers of Jesus of Nazareth do neither of these things? After Jesus was executed, his followers didn't give up the revolution; nor did they choose another leader from the same would-be royal family. Why not?

Here's a second puzzle. Jews regularly visited the grave of someone they had loved, to pray and to grieve. They would do this especially when the person had been a great hero or leader. You may have seen this on the news, in November 1995, when thousands of Jews flocked to pray at the grave of Yitzhak Rabin after his assassination. But there is no evidence that anyone ever went to Jesus' tomb for this purpose—except on the Sunday morning immediately after his death, when they got more than they bargained for.

Here's a third puzzle: the very word 'resurrection'. Most Jews at that time believed that God would raise all his people to new life, when he finally changed the whole world and established justice and peace for Israel in particular. That was what 'the resurrection' would mean. Nobody imagined that 'the resurrection' would ever refer to the rising to life of one person in the middle of history.

So why did Jesus' first followers insist that that was what had happened? Why didn't the story end when Jesus was crucified?

Why didn't they run away, go back to their fishing, give up the struggle? Alternatively, if they wanted to carry on with the kingdom-movement, why didn't they take one of Jesus' close relatives and propose him as the new Messiah, replacing the one who had just so obviously failed?

After all, Jesus' brother James was the great leader at the centre of the early church in Jerusalem, for thirty years after Jesus' death, until he too was murdered by the authorities. But nobody ever suggested that James was the Messiah. No; they were quite unambiguous: Jesus was the Messiah. Yes, he had been crucified. Yes, that normally meant you were a failed messiah. But no, he hadn't failed. He was the real thing. The question presses on us from all sides: why did they think he was the Messiah after all?

Most Jews at that time believed that God would raise all his people to new life, when he finally changed the whole world and established justice and peace for Israel in *particular. That was what 'the resurrection' would mean. Nobody imagined that 'the resurrection' would ever refer to the rising to life of one person in the middle of history.*

Why carry on?

Now many people have come up with many different answers. The bookshops and bookshelves are full of them.

But the early Christians give one answer, and only one. This is what they said: three days after Jesus' execution and burial, he was raised to bodily life again, leaving an empty tomb behind him.

Jesus' followers weren't expecting him to die in the first place; when he did, they certainly weren't expecting him to rise again.

They knew as well as we do that things like that just don't happen. When people died they stayed dead, in first-century Palestine just as much as in the technological twentieth century. Jesus' followers weren't expecting him to die in the first place; when he did, they certainly weren't expecting him to rise again. Yet they said, loud and clear, that that was what had happened.

The stories they told about Jesus' resurrection are mostly quite breathless and artless (Mark 16; Matthew 28; Luke 24; John 20—21). They are mostly much more like quick eye-witness sketches, with the details not even tidied up, than like carefully drawn portraits.

An exception to this is the story of the two disciples on the road to Emmaus (Luke 24:13–35). They were walking home, deeply sad and troubled, believing their leader to be dead and gone. They were joined by a stranger, who professed not to know what was going on. When they told him, he began to explain to them, working from the biblical texts they already knew, that this had been God's secret plan all along, to liberate Israel and the world, by means of the Messiah suffering, dying, and rising again.

Their hearts (as they said later) burned within them, as they began to realize the great possibility that after all his death might have been, so to speak, God's secret weapon—the last great move in the battle for the kingdom. God had been working in ways they never even dreamed of, even though they had been there all along in the scriptures.

Then, when they got home, they invited the stranger in. He quietly assumed the role of host, and broke the bread for their evening meal. They recognized him. It was Jesus himself. Then, as strangely as he had come, he disappeared again.

Now, clearly, Jesus' followers weren't just talking about a resuscitation. They certainly didn't think that Jesus had come back into

According to the Gospel of John, 'there was a garden in the place where he was crucified, and in the garden there was a new tomb in which no one had ever been laid. And so, because it was the Jewish day of Preparation, and the tomb was nearby, they laid Jesus there.' *(John 19:41-42)*

Jesus' followers weren't just talking about a resuscitation. They certainly didn't think that Jesus had come back into ordinary human life. No; they quickly came to the conclusion that he had gone through death and out the other side, into a new mode of human existence.

ordinary human life. No; they quickly came to the conclusion that he had gone *through* death and out the other side, into a new mode of human existence. He still had his human body, but it was changed, it was somehow different. It could be touched, but it could also go through locked doors. It could eat and drink, but it could also appear and disappear.

All the accounts suggest that the early Christians were as puzzled by this as we still are. But they are all quite clear that it happened. It wasn't a corporate hallucination. It wasn't a grief-induced fantasy. It was for real.

And they were all clear what it meant. It meant that the kingdom of God, which Jesus announced and enacted, had indeed come to birth. It means that the real return from exile had happened on what we now call Easter Day. Their hopes had indeed been fulfilled—but in a totally unexpected way. They said that the evil which had defaced and scarred the cosmos had in principle been defeated when Jesus died on the cross.

It meant that his followers now had a responsibility to tell the world that the new creation had begun; that justice and peace were now to be put into operation in all the world; and that all this could happen because the power of evil had been decisively broken.

We, too, need to be clear what this means. As far as the first Christians were concerned, it was the resurrection that meant they, and others, had to go on taking Jesus seriously. Without it, he remains a total enigma: a wonderful teacher, a great leader, a wise man of prayer—but ultimately a noble failure. With it, he stands at the great turning point of history, and beckons. And to those who see, and come, he points: points to the work he has for them to do; to implement his achievement; to take the news of his victory over evil and death to the ends of the earth. God knows we still need it.

7

God with a Human Face

FACING PAGE
da Mellozzo: 'The Redeemer'
Jesus redeems or makes good the relationship between people and God.

If then there is any encouragement in Christ, any consolation from love, any sharing in the Spirit, any compassion and sympathy, make my joy complete: be of the same mind, having the same love, being in full accord and of one mind.

Do nothing from selfish ambition or conceit, but in humility regard others as better than yourselves. Let each of you look not to your own interests, but to the interests of others. Let the same mind be in you that was in Christ Jesus,

who, though he was in the form of God,
did not regard equality with God
as something to be exploited,
but emptied himself,
taking the form of a slave,
being born in human likeness.

And being found in human form,
he humbled himself
and became obedient to the point of death—
even death on a cross.
Therefore God also highly exalted him
and gave him the name
that is above every name,
so that at the name of Jesus
every knee should bend,
in heaven and on earth and under the earth,
and every tongue should confess
that Jesus Christ is Lord,
to the glory of God the Father.

PHILIPPIANS 2:1–11

Asking the hard questions about Jesus has been part of my job for nearly twenty years; mostly in a university setting, and now as Dean at Lichfield Cathedral.

When people discover my academic background, one of the questions I'm often asked is: Can you, as a historian, say that Jesus is God?

It's a good question! But the trouble with it is that it's the wrong way round.

As historians we know quite a lot about Jesus. We know when he lived and how he died. We know what he taught and the most important things he did. We know something at least of what he believed he had to do, and how he believed he had to do it.

But do we know enough about God to be able to complete the equation? When people ask the question, 'Is Jesus God?', they tend to assume that we know who *God* is; the question means, Can you fit Jesus into your God-picture? Well, the best Christian answer has always been: we *don't know*, off the top of our heads, exactly who God is; but we can discover him by looking at Jesus. You could say that at the heart of the Christian faith is the view, not that Jesus is more or less like God, or part of God, but that the being we refer to as 'God' was, and is, fully present, and fully discoverable, in and as Jesus of Nazareth.

When people ask the question, 'Is Jesus God?', they tend to assume that we know who God is; the question means, Can you fit Jesus into your God-picture? Well, the best Christian answer has always been: we don't know, off the top of our heads, exactly who God is; but we can discover him by looking at Jesus.

What kind of God?

That's quite a big idea to get our heads round. For many people, the word 'God' means a remote being, detached from the world, defined by a set of dry dogmas, maintaining a dignified distance from the rough-and-tumble of human life. Now, if you say 'Is Jesus God?', referring to *that* god, the answer would have to be 'no'. It would always be nonsense to imagine that Jesus and *that* god are somehow to be identified.

But why *should* we believe in a god like that?

Supposing instead you start off with the God that Jesus knew about, the God Jesus discovered in the Hebrew scriptures, the passionate and compassionate God. What might *that* God look like?

Well, that God is big enough to be the creator of the world, and tender enough to take

IN:RI

Mantegna: 'The Crucifixion'
The letters above Christ's head are the initials of the Latin words for 'Jesus of Nazareth, King of the Jews', the inscription that Pilate had ordered to be placed there *(John 19:19-22)*.

care of the young birds when they call on him. He hears the cry of his people when they are in slavery. He is the God of whom the prophet Isaiah says, 'The Lord has made bare his holy arm'—which in plain English means 'the true God has rolled up his sleeves to come and sort things out himself.'

Now if you start off with *this* God, and say 'what might *this* God look like if he were to become human?'—then the life, and particularly the death, of Jesus of Nazareth, might show the true God as a human being, or in traditional Christian language, God incarnate.

This is a God with a human face: the face of Jesus of Nazareth, most clearly recognizable as God when he dies on the cross, sharing and bearing the weight of the world's evil and pain.

This, moreover, is a God who became human *without doing violence to his own inner essential nature*. The true God is the God of sovereign love; and it's a contradiction in terms to suppose that love will remain uninvolved, or detached, or impersonal. The true God isn't a vaguely beneficial gas. He wears a human face, crowned with thorns.

And if we think back through the *life* of Jesus, as we've been doing in this book, and through the events that led to his death, we can see that Jesus wasn't concerned about a mere set of dogmas, or abstract teachings about a remote God.

This was flesh-and-blood, a human being aflame with the love of God, putting that love into practice wherever human beings were in need. This was immediate, and vital, and deeply personal.

The original Jesus

I believe that the closer we get to the original Jesus—to the storytelling Jesus, the healing Jesus, the welcoming Jesus, the Jesus who declared God's judgment on those who rejected the way of peace and justice—the closer we come to the kingdom-of-God Jesus, the closer we are to recognizing the face of the living God.

For many people today, this move is a bit radical, a bit threatening; so they prefer to back off, to see Jesus as simply, at best, a signpost to God, the revealer of God, the teacher of timeless truths, someone who provokes us into thinking differently and perhaps even into living differently.

The closer we get to the original Jesus—to the story-telling Jesus, the healing Jesus, the welcoming Jesus, the Jesus who declared God's judgment on those who rejected the way of peace and justice...the closer we are to recognizing the face of the living God.

We can contain that sort of Jesus; he's not particularly disturbing, and the God of whom he speaks is quite far off and doesn't make too many immediate demands on us. We can quite easily make this Jesus, and this God, support our own favourite agendas. That's an old game.

But the real Jesus won't let us get away with that. People often say that first-century Jews didn't have any idea of 'incarnation'—that nobody was walking around supposing that God could become human. It is then concluded that neither Jesus nor his first followers could have had any such idea. It must be a later corruption, they say.

But this isn't the case. The Jews had several symbols which spoke of their God, the creator, the living God, coming to dwell in their midst and to rescue and save them.

They believed that the divine Wisdom lived amongst God's people, to point them in the right way. Jesus acted and taught as if he were that Wisdom.

When somebody asks me, 'Was Jesus God?' I usually turn the question around. 'Is it true that the living God was uniquely and personally present in Jesus?'

They believed that the living God was present in the Law which he had given, to gather his people and guide them in the right way. Jesus lived and taught as if he were the true Law, the true lawgiver, and the true gathering-point of God's people.

They believed that the living God lived, supremely, in the temple in Jerusalem. Jesus acted and spoke as if he was called to do and be what the temple was and did.

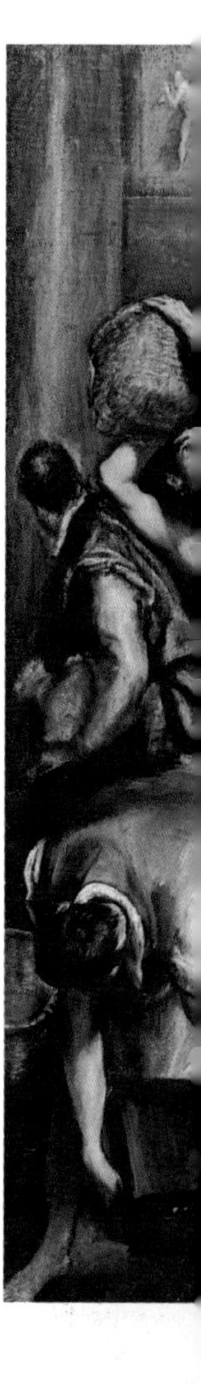

If we see somebody behaving pompously and arrogantly, we sometimes say 'He thinks he's God Almighty.' But that's a gross slur on God. Christianity focusses on a young Jew telling stories about the kingdom of God, healing the sick, confronting the powerful, dying under the weight of the world's pain, and rising again having defeated death itself; and Christianity says: '*That's* what it means to be God.'

So, when somebody asks me, 'Was Jesus God?' I usually turn the question around. 'Is it true that the living God was uniquely and personally present in Jesus?'

El Greco: 'Christ driving the traders from the temple'

A personal question

But the answer to that question can't remain simply an abstract theory, a detached doctrine. If you say 'no' to it, you are saying that Jesus was deluded; at best a tragic and noble failure, at worst a great charlatan and deceiver. You aren't staying neutral; you're looking at Jesus of Nazareth, and saying he was deeply mistaken.

But if you say 'yes' to it, you're committing yourself to a journey: a journey of exploration into God through exploring Jesus—his life, his teaching, his death and his resurrection.

If, as the apostle Paul says, 'in Christ God was reconciling the world to himself', then those who find themselves drawn into the love of this God must themselves join in the work of reconciliation...

From now on, therefore, we regard no one from a human point of view; even though we once knew Christ from a human point of view, we know him no longer in that way. So if anyone is in Christ, there is a new creation: everything old has passed away; see, everything has become new! All this is from God, who reconciled us to himself through Christ, and has given us the ministry of reconciliation; that is, in Christ God was reconciling the world to himself, not counting their trespasses against them, and entrusting the message of reconciliation to us. So we are ambassadors for Christ, since God is making his appeal through us; we entreat you on behalf of Christ, be reconciled to God.

2 CORINTHIANS 5:16–20

And that journey can neither be private nor self-centred. You see, if we start the journey by recognizing the rich, forgiving, healing love of the true God in the face of Jesus Christ, then to continue the journey means to join in with God's work of healing and love in the world. If, as the apostle Paul says, 'In Christ God was reconciling the world to himself', then those who find themselves drawn into the love of this God must themselves join in God's work of reconciliation.

You see, when we explore the question about Jesus and God, we discover another question: What might it look like today if people were captivated by the Spirit of this Jesus? At its best, the church consists of people who are struggling to answer that—not just in words, but in stories, and symbols, and actions—in their everyday lives.

That's how the Jesus who lived in real history 2000 years ago is alive and active in real history today.

This beautifully illuminated frontispiece to the Celtic Gospels manuscript called the Book of Kells makes use of the four traditional emblems of the Gospel writers: the man (Matthew), the lion (Mark), the ox (Luke) and the eagle (John).

Part 2

Reading the Gospels with Both Eyes Open

8

Getting to Grips with the Gospels

After looking at Jesus in his historical context, you may well be asking: how can I follow all this up? How can I find out more about Jesus, and fill in some of the gaps? How can I get to grips with the material for myself?

Part of the answer will always be: join in with other people who are trying to follow Jesus. Meet with them, worship with them, pray with them, discuss with them. Following Jesus is never simply a solo effort. What's more, it's never simply an activity of the mind, divorced from the rest of human life.

Taking Jesus seriously

But in our culture today it is very important to stress that the mind, the understanding, the serious and intelligent grasp of things, really does matter as well. Some try to dismiss this, by saying that people either have 'faith' or they don't have 'faith'—so there's nothing really to talk about. The whole Christian tradition stands over against that. Jesus announced his message in public. His first followers did the same. Anyone wanting to follow him today would need to have such a good grasp on what they believe, and why they believe it, that they could copy the first Christians and give a reason for their faith.

That means reading, and studying, the earliest evidence about Jesus.

And that means the Gospels.

In the second part of this book I want to introduce you to the two very different worlds that the Gospels come from, so that you can appreciate why they are what they are, and so that you can read them intelligently and profitably. Only so can you grow and develop in your understanding of who Jesus was, why he did and said what he did and said, and what it might mean for people today. Obviously a book like this is only a start. That's why I am including a short reading list of books which might help you to follow up on particular matters. But I hope this will get you going on the right track.

Naive or sceptical?

Pick up a newspaper. Read the first article that catches your eye. Do you believe it? 'It must be true; I read it in the papers.' That's an old joke; we all know that half of what gets into the media is distorted, or even sometimes downright fiction. When you know something about the events the papers report, you spot at once that they've got at least some details wrong. But many people, reading anything from the newspapers to the Bible, assume without question that every word is simply a description of actual fact. If they discover it isn't after all, they feel cheated, let down.

Many readers of the Gospels, particularly within devout Christian contexts, assume that they tell us the same as we would have got if someone had been following Jesus around with a camcorder. You don't have to read very far, though, before you discover that this can't be so.

Many readers of the Gospels, particularly within devout Christian contexts, assume that they tell us the same as we would have got if someone had been following Jesus around with a camcorder. You don't have to read very far, though, before you discover that this can't be so. Take the accounts in all four Gospels of Jesus' trial before the High Priest. Even if you say that each Gospel has recorded something that really happened, you quickly discover that they each have their own angle, the bits they put in which the others don't. None of them represents the whole scene that you get by trying (it's difficult) to put them all together.

Take the accounts one by one at each stage of the story and you'll see what I mean.

Matthew says that Jesus was taken to Caiaphas the High Priest (Mark and Luke don't name him); John, that he was taken to Annas, the father-in-law of Caiaphas. John and Luke then tell the story of Peter's denial, which Matthew and Mark reserve for after the 'trial'.

Duccio: 'Christ before Annas and the denial of Peter'

Many readers of the Gospels... assume that they tell us the same as we would have got if someone had been following Jesus around with a video camera or a tape recorder. You don't have to read very far, though, before you discover that this can't be so. Take the account in all four Gospels of Jesus' trial before the High Priest. Even if you say that each Gospel has recorded something that really happened, you quickly discover that they each have their own angle...

1 *Those who had arrested Jesus took him to Caiaphas the high priest, in whose house the scribes and the elders had gathered.*

2 *But Peter was following him at a distance, as far as the courtyard of the high priest; and going inside, he sat with the guards in order to see how this would end.*

3 *Now the chief priests and the whole council were looking for false testimony against Jesus so that they might put him to death, but they found none, though many false witnesses came forward. At last two came forward and said, 'This fellow said, "I am able to destroy the temple of God and to build it in three days." '*

4 *The high priest stood up and said, 'Have you no answer? What is it that they testify against you?' But Jesus was silent. Then the high priest said to him, 'I put you under oath before the living God, tell us if you are the Messiah, the Son of God.' Jesus said to him, 'You have said so. But I tell you,*

From now on you will see the Son of Man
seated at the right hand of Power
and coming on the clouds of heaven.'

Then the high priest tore his clothes and said, 'He has blasphemed! Why do we still need witnesses? You have now heard his blasphemy. What is your verdict?' They answered, 'He deserves death.'

5 *Then they spat in his face and struck him; and some slapped him, saying, 'Prophesy to us, you Messiah! Who is it that struck you?'*

6 *Now Peter was sitting outside in the courtyard. A servant-girl came to him and said, 'You also were with Jesus the Galilean.' But he denied it before all of them, saying, 'I do not know what you are talking about.' When he went out to the porch, another servant-girl saw him, and she said to the bystanders, 'This man was with Jesus of Nazareth.' Again he denied it with an oath, 'I do not know the man.' After a little while the bystanders came up and said to Peter, 'Certainly you are also one of them, for your accent betrays you.' Then he began to curse, and he swore an oath, 'I do not know the man!' At that moment the cock crowed. Then Peter remembered what Jesus had said: 'Before the cock crows, you will deny me three times.' And he went out and wept bitterly.*

MATTHEW 26:57–75

1 *They took Jesus to the high priest; and all the chief priests, the elders, and the scribes were assembled.*

2 *Peter had followed him at a distance, right into the courtyard of the high priest; and he was sitting with the guards, warming himself at the fire.*

3 *Now the chief priests and the whole council were looking for testimony against Jesus to put him to death; but they found none. For many gave false testimony against him, and their testimony did not agree. Some stood up and gave false testimony against him, saying, 'We heard him say, "I will destroy this temple that is made with hands, and in three days I will build another, not made with hands." ' But even on this point their testimony did not agree.*

4 *Then the high priest stood up before them and asked Jesus, 'Have you no answer? What is it that they testify against you?'*

But he was silent and did not answer. Again the high priest asked him, 'Are you the Messiah, the Son of the Blessed One?' Jesus said, 'I am; and

"you will see the Son of Man
seated at the right hand of the Power",
and "coming with the clouds of heaven." '

Then the high priest tore his clothes and said, 'Why do we still need witnesses? You have heard his blasphemy! What is your decision?' All of them condemned him as deserving death.

5 *Some began to spit on him, to blindfold him, and to strike him, saying to him, 'Prophesy!' The guards also took him over and beat him.*

6 *While Peter was below in the courtyard, one of the servant-girls of the high priest came by. When she saw Peter warming himself, she stared at him and said, 'You also were with Jesus, the man from Nazareth.' But he denied it, saying, 'I do not know or understand what you are talking about.' And he went out into the forecourt. Then the cock crowed. And the servant-girl, on seeing him, began again to say to the bystanders, 'This man is one of them.' But again he denied it. Then after a little while the bystanders again said to Peter, 'Certainly you are one of them; for you are a Galilean.' But he began to curse, and he swore an oath, 'I do not know this man you are talking about.' At that moment the cock crowed for the second time. Then Peter remembered that Jesus had said to him, 'Before the cock crows twice, you will deny me three times.' And he broke down and wept.*

MARK 14:53–72

1 *Then they seized him and led him away, bringing him into the high priest's house.*

2 *But Peter was following at a distance. When they had kindled a fire in the middle of the courtyard and sat down together, Peter sat among them.*

6 *Then a servant-girl, seeing him in the firelight, stared at him and said, 'This man also was with him.' But he denied it, saying, 'Woman, I do not know him.' A little later someone else, on seeing him, said, 'You also are one of them.' But Peter said, 'Man, I am not!' Then about an hour later yet another kept insisting, 'Surely this man also was with him; for he is a Galilean.' But Peter said, 'Man, I do not know what you are talking about!' At that moment, while he was still speaking, the cock crowed. The Lord turned and looked at Peter. Then Peter remembered the word of the Lord, how he had said to him, 'Before the cock crows today, you will deny me three times.' And he went out and wept bitterly.*

5 *Now the men who were holding Jesus began to mock him and beat him; they also blindfolded him and kept asking him, 'Prophesy! Who is it that struck you?' They kept heaping many other insults on him.*

4 *When day came, the assembly of the elders of the people, both chief priests and scribes, gathered together, and they brought him to their council. They said, 'If you are the Messiah, tell us.' He replied, 'If I tell you, you will not believe; and if I question you, you will not answer. But from now on the Son of Man will be seated at the right hand of the power of God.' All of them asked, 'Are you, then, the Son of God?' He said to them, 'You say that I am.' Then they said, 'What further testimony do we need? We have heard it ourselves from his own lips!'*
LUKE 22:54–71

1 *First they took him to Annas, who was the father-in-law of Caiaphas, the high priest that year. Caiaphas was the one who had advised the Jews that it was better to have one person die for the people.*

2 *Simon Peter and another disciple followed Jesus. Since that disciple was known to the high priest, he went with Jesus into the courtyard of the high priest, but Peter was standing outside at the gate. So the other disciple, who was known to the high priest, went out, spoke to the woman who guarded the gate, and brought Peter in.*

6 *The woman said to Peter, 'You are not also one of this man's disciples, are you?' He said, 'I am not.' Now the slaves and the police had made a charcoal fire because it was cold, and they were standing round it and warming themselves. Peter also was standing with them and warming himself.*

4 *Then the high priest questioned Jesus about his disciples and about his teaching. Jesus answered, 'I have spoken openly to the world; I have always taught in synagogues and in the temple, where all the Jews come together. I have said nothing in secret. Why do you ask me? Ask those who heard what I said to them; they know what I said.' When he had said this, one of the police standing nearby struck Jesus on the face, saying, 'Is that how you answer the high priest?' Jesus answered, 'If I have spoken wrongly, testify to the wrong. But if I have spoken rightly, why do you strike me?' Then Annas sent him bound to Caiaphas the high priest.*

6 *Now Simon Peter was standing and warming himself. They asked him, 'You are not also one of his disciples, are you?' He denied it and said, 'I am not.' One of the slaves of the high priest, a relative of the man whose ear Peter had cut off, asked, 'Did I not see you in the garden with him?' Again Peter denied it, and at that moment the cock crowed.*
JOHN 18:13–27

van Honthorst: 'Christ before the High Priest'

Luke then has those holding Jesus mock him as a false prophet, before, at daybreak, gathering the chief priests and scribes and holding a meeting of the Sanhedrin. Matthew and Mark imply that the trial goes ahead at night.

Matthew and Mark describe false witnesses accusing Jesus; Matthew's account is shorter (a regular feature where these two closely overlap). Both end with the High Priest asking Jesus if he is the Messiah, to which Jesus answers 'You said so' (Matthew) or 'I am' (Mark). At this point Luke joins the account again: he has Jesus giving a fuller but more cryptic response ('if I tell you, you won't believe, and if I question you, you won't answer'). In each of the three, Jesus continues with a clear allusion to (among other texts) Daniel 7, with its prediction of the vindication, the coming in glory to God, of 'one like a son of man'. Matthew and Mark have him say that Caiaphas will witness this vindication; Luke, that 'from now on' the vindication will have taken place. Luke then has the court ask Jesus again 'You are the son of God, then?' ('Son of God' was a title for the Messiah.) This is the point, in Luke, where Jesus combines the words given in Matthew and Mark to the earlier question ('You say that I am').

The High Priest then tears his clothes (Matthew and Mark), declaring that no further witnesses are needed (Matthew, Mark and Luke). The court agrees that Jesus deserves death (Matthew and Mark). This is the point in Matthew and Mark at which Jesus is mocked as a false prophet, and at which Peter denies Jesus three times. (In John, Peter denies Jesus once prior to the hearing before Annas, and twice afterwards.) After this, Matthew, Mark and Luke all have Jesus taken to Pilate.

John, meanwhile, has a longer conversation, in which Annas, described as the High Priest, asks Jesus about his followers and his teaching. Jesus' reply earns him a blow on the face, the legitimacy of which he challenges; Annas then sends him to Caiaphas, whence he is taken, without more reported questioning, to Pilate.

Where does all this take us? My point is not that the discrepancies prove all the accounts to be fictitious. That would be an astonishingly naive response to the evidence. Indeed, the very discrepancies read, if anything, much more like eye-witness reports of the same confused, swift and frightening events than like an attempt, long afterwards, to construct a piece of fiction out of theological motivations.

It is not that the discrepancies prove all the accounts to be fictitious. Indeed, the very discrepancies read much more like eye-witness reports of the same events.

My point, rather, is that even if you were to manage to produce a harmonized account in which every detail of every Gospel somehow fitted together, you would have succeeded in proving, not that any of them had given you a full and accurate transcript of everything that took place, but that none of them had done so. The accounts do not permit a simplistic realism ('it all happened exactly like that') any more than a simplistic cynicism ('nothing like that happened at all').

One other thing has already emerged from this very brief study of one short passage. Matthew, Mark and Luke are much more like one another (with Matthew and Mark often being particularly close) than any of them are like John. John, here as frequently, goes his own way; the others can be lined up and studied side by side, which gets them their name, 'the *synoptic* Gospels'.

Different theories have been offered to explain the large differences between John and the synoptics. A view which was popular a century ago, and which is still favoured in several quarters, is that John is basically a theologically inspired fiction, giving us a picture of 'the Christ of faith' rather than of the Jesus of history. Several scholars, however, have argued at length that John, though clearly an astonishingly deep thinker and theologian, was also in touch with very early traditions which have as good a claim to be taken seriously as history as those in the other three Gospels. It is not possible to pronounce on this question here; but the reader coming to the documents for the first time may like to know that, just as some have argued that John, though clearly a theologian, is also in touch with history, so most scholars today would say that the synoptic Gospels, though rooted in history, are also works of powerful and intricate theology.

So what? A good many biblical scholars during the last two centuries have done what readers of newspapers do when they feel cheated after discovering that something isn't after all 'straight fact'. They go to the other extreme, of

	60BC	**63** Roman general Pompey conquers Palestine, enters Jerusalem
	50BC	
31 Antony and Cleopatra defeated by Octavian at Battle of Actium. Egypt loses its independence to Rome	40BC	**37** Herod the Great appointed 'King of the Jews' by Roman senate
30 Augustus becomes Roman emperor	30BC	
	20BC	
	10BC BC	**5/4** Birth of Jesus **4** Death of Herod the Great
	AD	
14 Death of Augustus: accession of Tiberius	10AD	**18** Caiaphas made high priest in Jerusalem
	20AD	**26** Pontius Pilate becomes governor of Judea **27-30** Ministry of Jesus
37 Death of Tiberius: accession of Caligula	30AD	**30** Jesus' death and resurrection **31/33** Conversion of Paul
41 Death of Caligula: accession of Claudius **49** Claudius expels Jews from Rome	40AD	**46-48** Paul's first missionary journey
54 Death of Claudius: accession of Nero	50AD	**49-51** Paul in Corinth
69 'Year of four emperors' **70** Titus captures and destroys Jerusalem	60AD 70AD	**64-66** Deaths of Peter and Paul **66-70** Jewish War against Rome

cynicism or scepticism. They assume that whatever they find in the text must be distorted, twisted, slanted, biassed, or even made up out of thin air.

In recent years one group of American scholars in particular, calling itself 'The Jesus Seminar', has turned this sort of scepticism into an art form. They have produced books and articles in which they claim 'scientific' grounds for saying that Jesus never said, or did, about 80 per cent of the things which the Gospels say he said and did. They cast great doubt on the canonical Gospels of Matthew, Mark, Luke and John, called 'canonical' because they are part of what Christians recognize as the authoritative 'canon' of scripture. They claim that a very different book, known as 'The Gospel of Thomas', gives us as good, or better, access to Jesus, even though some of the sayings it records are very different from those in the four mainstream Gospels. The 'Jesus Seminar' distrusts the 'canonical' Gospels precisely because they are authorized by the mainstream churches of the last two thousand years (so they are 'biassed').

A good many scholars on both sides of the Atlantic, however, have been very sceptical, in turn, of the 'Jesus Seminar' and its decisions. Those decisions, in fact, seem to have as much to do with the Seminar's hatred of certain types of Christianity, not least fundamentalism, as with serious historical research. Some of the most serious and learned contemporary writers about early Christianity, such as Martin Hengel of Tübingen University, take a very different line, offering a far more positive reconstruction of Christian origins, and of what we can know and say about Jesus. In what follows I shall propose a quite different way of understanding the Gospels to that which the 'Jesus Seminar' suggest, one which in my view (argued in detail in some of my other books) has a far better claim to be seriously historical and scholarly.

The two worlds of the Gospels

The Middle East has always been a place where different cultures meet. Sometimes they dance together; sometimes, alas, they fight. Always the mix is rich, complex, fascinating. Try understanding the politics of any one Middle-Eastern country today, and you'll see what I mean.

In the first century AD, the two great cultures in Palestine were Jewish and Greek; only now the Greek was overlaid with the Roman. Alexander the Great had conquered Palestine in 332BC; from that day on, Greek was everybody's second language, much as English is for half the world today. But the Greek empire had faded. It had been succeeded by periods of Egyptian and Syrian rule, and a century of Jewish semi-independence. Then came the Romans. Building on the old classical Greek culture, they introduced a more ruthless system of government. They made a special concession, allowing the Jews to worship their own God in their own way, because they realized that the Jews were prepared to die rather than do anything else. But there wasn't much love lost between them.

Meanwhile, the Jews cherished their two-thousand-year-old history, culture, way of life and faith. They clung to it in good times and (particularly) in bad, believing that since their God was the creator of the whole world he would one day deliver them from the pagans (by which they meant anyone who didn't worship their God—in other words, more or less the rest of the world). They had a highly-developed sense of national identity, forged in the fires of persecution. They had an astonishingly rich religion, with poetical songs that are still sung today all around the world, stories to keep you on the edge of your seat, and vivid prophecies about the great day that was coming when the true God would rescue his people and create a world full of justice and peace. They had an astonishingly detailed code for everyday life, based (they believed) on instructions from God himself, more than a thousand years before. They had all sorts of wonderful festivals, celebrating the great things their God had done for them in the past. They had a capital city which was hailed as one of the most beautiful places in the world. And in the middle of the city was the temple where, they believed, the living God had promised to dwell with his people.

In the Middle East in the first century, these two great cultures—Greece and Rome combined on the one hand, and Judaism on the other—met, fought, arranged truces, lived uneasily with one another, learnt to speak parts of each others' languages, tried to dominate or convert or escape from each other.

That was the world in which Christianity was born. That was the world in which the Gospels were written, in which they made sense.

That is the world we need to understand if we want to read the Gospels with both eyes open.

A two-eyed reading of the Gospels

The Gospels were conceived and written with two purposes, both equally important.

The Gospels were written, first, *to tell the story of Jesus.*

Some scholars have tried to suggest that the evangelists (the Gospel-writers) weren't actually much interested in Jesus himself, or that they didn't have access to much real information about him, or that they weren't trying in any sense to write 'biography'. Instead, such scholars (including many in the 'Jesus Seminar') think the Gospels were simply the expression of early Christian faith and experience, in which stories 'about' Jesus weren't anything of the kind. They were just miniature novels, designed to speak of, and to commend, the speaker's Christian faith.

This theory sounds sophisticated, but actually it's quite shallow. The fact that the evangelists were addressing their own world doesn't mean that they weren't talking about Jesus. As we shall see presently, the Gospels only make sense if they are read as describing Jesus himself.

> *There is no such thing as a point of view which is nobody's point of view. Nobody is ever a fly on the wall. All storytelling is storytelling with a purpose. The Gospels are no exception.*

But, second, it is of course true that the Gospels were written *to address the evangelists' contemporaries*. They weren't attempting to give you what you'd have got from our hypothetical character following Jesus round with a camcorder. In fact, no historian, no reporter, nobody ever tells things 'just like they happened'. All stories about all events involve the story-teller in selection, collection, arrangement and hence 'interpretation'. That doesn't mean the whole thing is a pack of lies. It just means there is no such thing as a point of view which is nobody's point of view. Nobody is ever a fly on the wall. All storytelling is story-telling with a purpose. The Gospels are no exception.

Despite what some scholars have tried to argue, we actually know a lot more about Jesus than we do about the early church.

To read the Gospels, then, we must continually be alert *both* for the question 'what is this telling us about Jesus?' and for the question 'what is the evangelist trying to say, through this story about Jesus, to his own contemporaries?' This means working out why the evangelist has selected and arranged his material in the way he has, and seeing whether that forms something of a pattern which tells us about his own agenda, the points he wanted to emphasize. That's by no means easy. Despite what some scholars have tried to argue, we actually know a lot more about Jesus than we do about the early church. But sometimes, as we discover how the evangelist was addressing his contemporaries with the original message about Jesus, we begin to discover, too, how he might be addressing us today. So the effort can be worthwhile.

Reading between the lines

There are lots of other ways in which the Gospels are sometimes read. Some scholars have tried to read between the lines, to see what the stories about Jesus meant when they were circulating by word of mouth in the period between the events themselves and the time, a generation or so later, when they were written down. This task (known as 'form criticism',

Early church tradition maintained that Mark's Gospel was based on recollections dictated to him by Peter, as depicted in this ancient ivory relief.

because it looks at the 'form' of the different stories and tries to deduce things from it) is sometimes possible, and sometimes quite illuminating. But it isn't an easy task.

Equally, lots of scholars have laboured to try to solve the puzzle of how the Gospels as we have them relate to one another, and to hypothetical 'sources' that may lie behind them. This relates particularly to Matthew, Mark and Luke, which, placed side by side, have quite a lot of material in common. Most scholars used to agree that Mark was written first, and that Matthew and Luke used Mark on the one hand, and on the other hand a source, now lost, called 'Q' (standing for the German word *Quelle*, which means 'source'). Probably 70 per cent of New Testament scholars still believe some version of this theory, but the remaining 30 per cent either don't believe it or would say they aren't sure.

People used to suppose that a great deal hung on a decision about this 'source criticism'. If only we could find our way back to the original sources, they thought, we would get that much closer to Jesus.

Things aren't actually that easy. The world in which Jesus and his first followers lived was what we call an 'oral' culture, not a 'writing' culture. People relied on the spoken word much more than on written texts. This doesn't mean that everything was as fuzzy and fluid as things would be in our culture if we relied on memory for everything. There are two reasons why, in fact, oral tradition was very reliable in those days and in that situation.

First, people in those days really used their memories, in a way which we, with four hundred years of print and forty of computers, have almost completely forgotten how to do. Think of the surprise a schoolchild feels on discovering that, at the end of rehearsals for the school play, he or she knows the entire thing by heart.

Second, when something forms an important part of your world, your life, your culture, you tell it and retell it—and you remember it, and don't change it. Think of what would happen if someone took one of the songs of a cultural hero like Bob Dylan—say, 'Blowing in the wind'—and changed one of the lines. Everybody knows the words (especially those of us who grew up in the sixties); not because we've seen them written down, but because we've heard them and sung them. So it was for the early Christians: the stories of what Jesus had done and said were etched into their minds. They were the things that made them who they were. They wouldn't chop and change them at random.

When something forms an important part of your world, your life, your culture, you tell it and retell it—and you remember it, and don't change it.

So when we pick up the Gospels we have good reason to suppose that they intend to talk about Jesus, not just about their own situations; and that they have a good claim to be basically reliable. We must now look a bit more closely at those two worlds from which they came, and see where they fit, and how they were attempting to carve out space for a new worldview which would address both cultures with a new message.

9

The Jewish World of the Gospels

The Jewish world of Jesus' day was very much a storytelling world. Stories, as we saw in Part 1, are not just kids' stuff, pretty embroidery around the edges of serious abstract thought. Stories are dynamic and explosive. They do things; they change things; they make things.

The Jewish story and its retelling

In Jesus' world, some of the most important stories were designed to do something very specific: to change the way Jews thought about themselves and their present state, and to make a new world in which everything would be different. Most of these stories came from their

Bible (which we call the Old Testament); some, from more recent tradition. Again and again, they played the same tune. The pagan nations would trample upon Israel, enslaving and oppressing the people. Then Yahweh, her God, would remember the promises that he had made, and would act dramatically within history to rescue Israel, to set the people free, to show the world that he was the true God and they were his true people.

The best-known of these stories was the Exodus. Israel was enslaved in Egypt; God sent Moses to liberate her. The Israelites crossed the Red Sea on dry land, and made it home to the Promised Land. The pattern was repeated, particularly with the exile in Babylon roughly a thousand years later. The book of Esther tells of one particular incident, when the Jews were about to be massacred and were saved at the last minute. As recently as two hundred years before Jesus' day, the Jews were crushed by a megalomaniac king of Syria (Antiochus Epiphanes); but Judas Maccabeus managed (with, he would have said, the help of God) to overturn the pagan rule and establish Israel as a more or less free nation.

Stories are not just kids' stuff, pretty embroidery around the edges of serious abstract thought. Stories are dynamic and explosive. They do things; they change things; they make things.

In each of these cases—Exodus, Esther, and the Maccabean crisis—the memory was kept fresh not just by books, to be read by the learned, but by great festivals. In Britain to this day, every child knows who Guy Fawkes was, not because they've read in books about how he tried to blow up Parliament in 1605, but because every year, on the fifth of November, there are bonfire parties with fireworks. For more or less the same reason, every Jewish child knew (and knows to this day) about Moses and the Exodus, because of the festival of Passover; about Esther, because of the festival of Purim; about Judas Maccabeus, because of Hanukkah. These were their stories. The stories made them who they were.

And the stories all said: God would do it again. Here they were again, with the Romans doing to them what everybody else had done before. They must not only tell the story, they must live the story, and God would rescue them once more. Only this time he would do it (they believed) once and for all. God would be king, and they would be free for ever. That, as we saw in Part 1, was how they thought of their own history.

The Dead Sea Scrolls

One community in particular, in the Jewish world of Jesus' day, has left us a remarkable record of how they retold the Jewish story so as to include themselves within it. When the Dead Sea Scrolls were discovered in 1947 and subsequent years, they opened up to public gaze, for the first time since AD 68, the life of a little group who believed that they were the true Israel, and that Israel's God was about to act in history and vindicate them.

Some writers have from time to time made

grandiose claims about the Scrolls. They have suggested that the Dead Sea community had something to do with early Christianity; that Jesus was himself a member, perhaps the leader, of the community; that either John the Baptist, or James (Jesus' brother), or Paul, was involved with it. The Scrolls themselves, of course, say nothing of this. Since, however, they are written in a very oblique style, often interpreting biblical prophecies in what seem to us very fanciful ways, they open the door to modern writers with a fertile imagination. But serious scholarship, whether Jewish or Christian, Protestant or Catholic, believing, agnostic or atheist, has consistently denied that Jesus and early Christianity had anything directly to do with the Scrolls and the community that produced them.

In particular, there was not, and is not, any 'conspiracy' to hush up the Scrolls.

I received a letter in late 1995 from someone convinced that the Roman Catholic Church was responsible for suppressing the Scrolls, and asking why I and other church leaders didn't speak out to demand their publication. This was bizarre. By then, photographs of all the Scrolls that had been found had already been published; those that are big enough to be edited as texts (some are very tiny, with only a couple of letters) have been edited and translated, notably in a splendid volume produced by the Spanish scholar Florentino García Martínez. The Scrolls don't undermine Christianity. They don't even mention it.

A couple of scholars (O'Callaghan and Thiede) have claimed that fragments of the New Testament have turned up among the Scrolls. They argue that Cave 7 (out of the eleven caves in which documents were found) contains various Christian writings, and that one fragment in particular contains a small part (a few letters) of Mark's Gospel. If this is true, it would obviously have enormous implications not only for understanding Qumran, but also for the Gospels: it would mean that Mark, at least, was written well before AD68, when the Romans destroyed Qumran. But the great majority of scholars who have studied the fragments remain unconvinced that they have anything to do with the New Testament.

The Dead Sea Scrolls don't undermine Christianity. They don't even mention it.

The Scrolls reveal a community that is a sort of second cousin to Christianity.

The Scrolls do, however, shed a flood of light on early Christianity, from one particular angle. They show how, within the turbulent world of first-century Judaism, a group that believed God was acting in history to liberate his people, and was doing so in and through their community, might retell the story of God and his people so as to include themselves within it. They interpreted their scriptures as prophecies that had begun to come true within their own history. They were, so they believed, the advance guard of the community of the new covenant, the real people of God. Soon God would act to defeat the pagans, and the renegade Jews (the Qumran group regarded all other Jews as renegade, particularly the regime in Jerusalem), and to establish them as the true Israel.

The Scrolls thus reveal a community that is a sort of second cousin to Christianity. Christians, too, believed that they were the true people of the one true God; that God had acted in history to establish them as such; that he would act again to confirm them as such. But there are significant differences. The early Christians believed, unlike the Scroll-writers, that the central and decisive event had already happened—in the events concerning Jesus. At the same time, when we compare the two bodies of literature, there are lots of similarities, family resemblances. Both communities sustained themselves by *retelling the story of God and Israel so as to include themselves within it, as part of the fulfilment of scriptural prophecy*. Thus, though the Scrolls do not mention Jesus or Christianity, explicitly or in code, we can learn a lot in both directions by putting the two side by side.

Waiting for the climax

In particular, the Scrolls, and a good deal of other Jewish literature from what we call the Second Temple period (i.e. the last four hundred years BC, and the first hundred AD), speak of the living God getting ready to act in such a way that the only language one can use for it is dramatic, cosmic, and apocalyptic. They speak of the sun and moon being darkened, the stars falling from heaven, and so on.

When they do this, they aren't giving a primitive sort of weather forecast. They don't expect their readers or hearers to imagine that the space-time universe is literally going to come to a full stop, with a Big Crunch, such as some scientists think may happen eventually. No: the Jews who use this sort of language (it goes back at least as far as passages like Isaiah 13) intend it to refer to events *within* what we call the space-time world, particularly the world of large-scale international events and politics. And they intend it to invest those events with their full significance.

An example may make this clear. When the Berlin Wall fell in 1989, political commentators naturally reached for dramatic language. It was, they said, an 'earth-shattering event'. They didn't mean there had been a literal earthquake. They meant that, at the social and political level, nothing in Europe would be the same again. It was the end of an era.

This is enormously important when learning to read the Gospels, which use this sort of language for two things in particular: the death and resurrection of Jesus, and the fall of Jerusalem (which Jesus predicted). When Jesus says things like 'They will see the Son of Man coming on the clouds with power and great glory' (Mark 13:26), it would be a mistake of the Berlin-Wall-and-earthquake sort to suppose he meant, or Mark meant, that people would one day see a human being, perhaps Jesus himself, floating downwards to earth, sitting on a cloud. The language in question is high-grade biblical imagery (from Daniel 7, actually) which is used to *describe* God's vindication of his true people, and to *invest* that event with its full significance. When God delivers his people, and defeats their enemies, this will be nothing less than a revelation of God himself in all his glory.

When Jesus says things like, 'They will see the Son of Man coming on the clouds with great power and glory', it would be a mistake... to suppose he meant, or Mark meant, that people would one day see a human being, perhaps Jesus himself, floating downwards to earth, sitting on a cloud. The language in question is high-grade biblical imagery (from Daniel 7, actually) which is used to describe God's vindication of his true people...

"As I looked,

"thrones were set in place,
  and the Ancient of Days took his seat.
His clothing was as white as snow;
  the hair of his head was white like wool.
His throne was flaming with fire,
  and its wheels were all ablaze.
A river of fire was flowing,
  coming out from before him.
Thousands upon thousands attended him;
  ten thousand times ten thousand stood before him.
The court was seated,
  and the books were opened.

"In my vision at night I looked, and there before me was one like a son of man, coming with the clouds of heaven. He approached the Ancient of Days and was led into his presence.

"He was given authority, glory and sovereign power; all peoples, nations and men of every language worshipped him. His dominion is an everlasting dominion that will not pass away, and his kingdom is one that will never be destroyed."

DANIEL 7:9–10, 13–14

As he came out of the temple, one of his disciples said to him, 'Look, Teacher, what large stones and what large buildings!' Then Jesus asked him, 'Do you see these great buildings? Not one stone will be left here upon another; all will be thrown down.'

When he was sitting on the Mount of Olives opposite the temple, Peter, James, John, and Andrew asked him privately, 'Tell us, when will this be, and what will be the sign that all these things are about to be accomplished?' Then Jesus began to say to them, 'Beware that no one leads you astray. Many will come in my name and say, 'I am he!' and they will lead many astray. When you hear of wars and rumours of wars, do not be alarmed; this must take place, but the end is still to come. For nation will rise against nation, and kingdom against kingdom; there will be earthquakes in various places; there will be famines. This is but the beginnings of the birthpangs...

'For in those days there will be suffering, such as has not been from the beginning of the creation that God created until now, no, and never will be. And if the Lord had not cut short those days, no one would be saved; but for the sake of the elect, whom he chose, he has cut short those days. And if anyone says to you at that time, "Look! Here is the Messiah!" or "Look! There he is!"—do not believe it. False messiahs and false prophets will appear and produce signs and omens, to lead astray, if possible, the elect. But be alert, I have already told you everything.

'But in those days, after that suffering,

the sun will be darkened
    and the moon will not give its light,
and the stars will be falling from heaven,
    and the powers in the heavens will be shaken.

'Then they will see "the Son of Man coming in clouds" with great power and glory.'

MARK 13:1–8, 19–26

The vivid language in which first-century Jews often wrote about what they expected God to do, which is shared by the Gospel writers, must be read as what it is, not as what it isn't. It isn't a set of predictions about the literal end of the space-time universe. It is a way of describing the events of Jesus' life, death and resurrection, and the promise of God's vindication of Jesus in and through the destruction of the regime that had opposed him (the Jerusalem temple and its present hierarchy), in a way which says: this is how the story of God's dealings with Israel and hence with the world is reaching its true climax. This isn't the end of the space-time world; it is the end of the present world order, and the ushering in of the new age that the prophets had promised long ago. It is the climax of history.

The Gospels should not be taken as free-standing compositions, to be read as though nothing else existed. They only make sense as the completion, the final chapter, of a great drama that had been running for two millennia.

The Gospels and the Jewish story

When we read the Gospels, then, we are reading books which tell the story of Jesus *as* the story of how the long drama between Israel and the covenant-God came to fulfilment and fruition. They should not be taken as free-standing compositions, to be read as though nothing else existed. They only make sense as the completion, the final chapter, of a great drama that had been running for two millennia.

That's why Matthew starts his Gospel with the long family tree that runs from Abraham to Jesus. He is summarizing the whole of Jewish history in a single page, as a way of telling 'the story so far'. That's why Mark begins his Gospel with two of the great prophecies from scripture, Isaiah 40 and Malachi 3. Those prophecies had been read for centuries as pointing forward to the great time that would come when Israel's God would comfort his people at last, when the long night of exile would be over and Israel would be free. That's why Luke begins his story in the temple, the place where the living God had promised to meet with his people; and with the story of John the Baptist, seen as the last great prophet in a long, long line. And that's why John, who takes the widest angle of all, begins his Gospel by echoing the opening words of the book of Genesis itself: 'In the beginning...' All these books were saying, in their own particular way: this is how the scriptures were fulfilled, how the story reached its climax, how God's long and chequered relationship with Israel, and with the world, was finally sorted out.

Notice what follows. Israel's whole worldview was from the beginning focussed on things that happen *in the real world*, the world of space and time. It was the Greeks, not the Jews, who thought that 'reality' was, so to speak, up in the air, a matter of ideas and beliefs rather than space-time-and-matter facts and events. They would have been perfectly happy with a world in which 'religious experience' was what counted and 'real life' could be left behind. That, in fact, is precisely what we find in some of the second- and third-level writings in the New Testament period, such as the so-called 'Gospel of Thomas' (which is in fact not a Gospel and not by Thomas). It conforms very well to the philosophy of some scholars at the present time, who don't like the idea of a God who acts within history, and prefer the idea of everyone having their own 'religious experience', of whatever sort. That chimes in with a good deal in contemporary culture. But it doesn't fit with the biblical worldview at all.

Israel's whole worldview was from the beginning focussed on things that happen in the real world, the world of space and time. It was the Greeks, not the Jews, who thought that 'reality' was, so to speak, up in the air, a matter of ideas and beliefs rather than space-time-and-matter facts and events.

On the contrary. The fact that the Gospel writers (not including 'Thomas') hook their stories in so thoroughly to the Jewish scriptures means that they were certainly and emphatically intending, despite what some scholars have tried to argue, to refer to *actual events that actually took place*. They were not writing 'code' for 'early Christian religious experience'. They were intending to talk about Jesus, what he did and what he said. And, as I suggested earlier, all the signs are that they pretty well succeeded. The Gospels are telling substantially *Jewish* stories about Jesus as the Jewish Messiah, the one in and through whom the story of Israel had finally come to its fulfilment. It was a surprising fulfilment; it didn't look like the sort of thing people had expected; but the whole of early Christianity was based on the belief that that was the correct way to understand the strange events that had happened, and were still happening.

One problem about the stories the Gospels tell of Jesus is that the Jesus they describe doesn't always fit with what the church at various periods has expected to find. He isn't 'gentle Jesus, meek and mild'; he isn't simply

Duccio: 'The Last Supper'

the teacher of lofty truths; he isn't instructing people on how to go to heaven when they die; he isn't teaching about a nonpolitical, non-earthly 'religion' or 'spirituality' through which people can escape the present world and experience a private religious glow inside. The Jesus of the Gospels—the original Jesus—is taking on the establishment and undermining it. He is behaving as though he's the rightful king of the Jews, when there is already a king of the Jews (Herod) who will be extremely angry if he finds out. He is announcing that Israel's God is becoming king, in and through his own work. He is inviting all and sundry to join in the kingdom-movement, by joining with him. He rides into Jerusalem and turns it upside down. He confronts the authorities, knowing precisely what they will do to him. And, when they are about to arrest him, he celebrates a strange meal with his followers which will serve as the pregnant clue, then and throughout subsequent history, to the meaning he is giving to his violent death. This is the story the evangelists all tell, in their own ways.

One problem about the stories the Gospels tell of Jesus is that the Jesus they describe doesn't always fit with what the church at various periods has expected to find.

Not surprisingly, it's such a huge and powerful story that many people find it hard to take, inside the church as well as outside it. The church, and the world, have developed ways of cutting the story down to size, to make it manageable, so it doesn't tower over us, dwarfing our little dramas and disturbing our little dreams. The scholarly efforts to belittle the story, to say that most of it was made up later, that Jesus was really just a great teacher or whatever, are simply part of the natural reaction to the fear that may come over us if we read the Gospels for all they're worth and discover that it was true, that Jesus of Nazareth really was the Messiah of Israel and hence the Lord of the world. This means that our own worldviews, including perhaps would-be Christian worldviews, might have to be remade once more around him. That's what you might let yourself in for when you read the Gospels as they were meant to be read. They ought to have a warning printed over the top of each page: Reading these Books Could Seriously Change Your Life.

The Gospels were not just written to describe events in the past. They were written to show that those events were relevant, indeed earth-shattering, worldview-challenging, and life-changing, in the present.

For the whole point about the Jewish worldview always was that when God acted for Israel, this would result in his acting for the whole world. The Gospels were written precisely in order to be part of that new movement. God, they believed, *had* acted for Israel once and for all, in Jesus. Jesus' followers were therefore charged with the responsibility of going into all the world and announcing the good news that the God of Israel had now acted to rescue not only Israel, but the whole world from its plight. The word 'Gospel' means 'good news', and it is indeed good news for everybody.

The Gospels, then, were not just written to describe events in the past. They were written to show that those events were relevant, indeed earth-shattering, worldview-challenging, and life-changing, in the present.

How, then, can we understand the Gospels within the other world which they inhabited, the world to which the early Christians took their good news—the world of Greece and Rome?

10 The Gospels: How, When and Why?

What do we know about how the Gospels got written? Frustratingly little. We don't have Matthew's diaries of how he went about collecting and arranging his material. We don't know where Mark was written. We don't know whether Luke really was, as is often thought, the companion of Paul. We don't know whether the 'Beloved Disciple', to whom the Fourth Gospel is ascribed (John 21:24), was really 'John' (in which case, which 'John'?) or someone else. None of the books name their authors; all the traditions about who wrote which ones are just that, traditions, from later on in the life of the church (beginning in the first half of the second century, about fifty years after the Gospels were written).

Dating the Gospels

That's another thing: we don't know *when* any of the Gospels was actually written. Scholars will pontificate and give you a precise date; and then you can listen to another scholar telling you with equal confidence something quite different. John A.T. Robinson argued twenty years ago that the whole New Testament was written before AD70; the rest of the scholarly community has, by and large, ignored him rather than refuting him. That's not to say he was right; only that the evidence is not substantial enough to make definite claims. The confidence with which some scholars pronounce that, for instance, Matthew and Luke were written in the eighties or nineties, and John some time between 90 and 110, is breathtaking. We know next to nothing about what Christianity was like in those decades. We certainly don't know enough to be able to date or place documents there. There are still a good many scholars, just as familiar with all the evidence as the ones I've alluded to, who think that Mark at least was written well before AD70, and that Matthew and Luke might have been written around then as well.

A particular argument has recently been advanced for firming up a date very early in this range of possibilities. Carsten Thiede, a papyrologist whom I mentioned earlier in connection with the scraps from Cave 7 at

Qumran, has argued that three scraps of papyrus, which originally were found in Egypt and are now in the library at Magdalen College, Oxford, are to be dated some time within the first Christian generation, perhaps in the middle or late sixties. The point is that these scraps definitely contain part of Matthew's Gospel. If they are to be dated that early it means that Matthew, which most scholars still think was written after Mark, was composed well within the lifetime of eyewitnesses of Jesus, pushing Mark even earlier.

Thiede's books make somewhat grandiose claims (as did the newspaper article with which the idea was first launched, on Christmas Eve 1994). He constantly suggests that the new theory will revolutionize Gospel studies, by dating Matthew (and hence at least Mark as well) several decades earlier than normally thought. He continually snipes away at other scholars who have taken it upon themselves to argue against the new theory, suggesting darkly that they are part of a scholarly conspiracy. There is a cover-up, he suggests, occasioned because of the number of cherished theories which will have to go out of the window if the Magdalen Papyrus were to be dated in the 60s. But none of this is really warranted.

The jury is still out on the precise dating of the papyrus in question. The comments of senior scholars in the field, however, suggest that it will be difficult if not impossible to shift the normal dating of the fragments, which puts them in the late second century AD. Despite the length of the book supposedly arguing for the early date of the fragment, hardly any of it actually deals with the date itself; and, when it comes, the argument turns out to be bound up with the identification of the Cave 7 fragments as part of Mark. This is like saying that one heavy weight hangs by a slender thread from another heavy weight, which in turn hangs by a slender thread from a shaky beam. It is just possible that the beam might hold; that both threads might not snap; and that, in time, firmer support might be found for the whole structure. But at the moment there is no reason to suppose it will be.

The crucial thing to say about this new theory is that *the argument for the substantial historicity and accuracy of the Gospels never depended on their dating, anyway*. True, lots of scholars have argued as though that was the case, with 'radical' scholars dating the Gospels late (and so darkly suggesting that they were all unreliable) and 'conservative' scholars dating them early (and so brightly suggesting that everything in them was taken down by eyewitnesses at the scene). But this is actually a mistake. The historicity and accuracy of the Gospels depends on our putting together the whole jigsaw of the first century, with Judaism and early Christianity side by side (and indeed confusingly intertwined with each other), and with Jesus as the middle term straddling both.

The argument for the substantial historicity and accuracy of the Gospels never depended on their dating... The historicity and accuracy of the Gospels depends on our putting together the whole jigsaw of the first century, with Judaism and early Christianity side by side... and with Jesus as the middle term straddling both.

The historicity of the Gospels depends, not on when they were written, but the historical plausibility of the picture they describe.

When we engage in this task, we discover, as I have argued in considerable detail elsewhere, that the stories about Jesus are not simply miscellaneous Jewish stories which happened to get attached to Jesus. Nor are they simply the retrojection of early Christian ideas and experience back on to him. They fit within the world of Judaism, and yet are clearly explosive within that world. They make sense as the reason why there was a 'Christianity' in the first place, yet they are significantly different from what we find even in the letters of Paul (our earliest written witness to Christianity). They belong, historically, only in the time of, and to the person of, Jesus himself. That is how, speaking as a historian, we can know that they really are about him.

At this point, someone may say: surely, if the Gospels are inspired scripture, breathed by God's Holy Spirit, they should be accurate in all ways? In a sense, yes. But beware. That argument is regularly used by people as an excuse for *not* reading the Gospels for all they're worth, but simply for reading them in a flat and naive way which fits with a modern Western worldview (albeit a would-be Christian one) rather than a truly Christian one. It is used, often, as an argument for treating the Gospels as a collection of proof-texts for a supposedly Christian worldview which in fact owes a great deal more to particular, and quite recent, traditions within the church, rather than to serious engagement with the God-breathed word itself. If we say that God inspired scripture, we are saying that God was involved in the rough-and-tumble, warts-and-all historical processes that led to us having these Gospels to read—not that they appeared from the sky one day, containing some sort of timeless truth divorced from history.

What, then, do we know about the origins of the Gospels? Not a lot, from one point of view. After a whole generation of scholarly activity trying to say when and where and by whom they were written, we are in several important respects no nearer to a solution. Quite simply, there isn't enough evidence to make a strong case one way or another.

But we can say *why* they were written. That, after all, is the really important thing. That's what we need to focus on if we're to get the best from them, if we are to allow them to lead us back both to Jesus himself and also out into the modern world. So let's take a look at them with this question in mind.

The eagle is the traditional emblem of the fourth Gospel writer. This engraving is from the reredos at Lichfield Cathedral, as are those on the following pages: the ox for Luke, the man for Matthew and the lion for Mark

Why John?

Let's begin with the Gospel most scholars (though not all) think was written last. The author (call him John for the sake of argument) actually tells us, in so many words, why he wrote his book: 'These things are written so that you may come to believe that Jesus is the Messiah, the Son of God, and that through believing you may have life in his name.' (John 20:31)

Frustratingly, there are two problems of text and translation at this point. Some manuscripts have 'that you may continue to believe' instead of 'that you may come to believe'; it's one small letter in the Greek, but it makes quite a difference, the difference between faith being *generated* and faith being *sustained*. However, the underlying point is clearly the same: by the end of reading this book, people should be believing that Jesus is the Messiah, whether or not they did before.

But then we meet the second problem. The Greek could, and perhaps should, be translated, not 'that Jesus is the Messiah', etc., but rather 'that the Messiah is Jesus'. In other words, it may not be starting with Jesus and showing that he is the Messiah; it may be starting with the idea of messiahship and showing that the Messiah really is Jesus. But, again, the underlying point is clear. Jesus is the Messiah; the Messiah is Jesus. By the time you're through, the two are identical. Believe it, says John; that way you will have 'life', which we know from the whole book means life in all its fulness, life which transcends ordinary human life, life which will continue in glory beyond the grave.

In other words, John's Gospel is written to say something about Jesus *and* something specific to the readers. They are not just to be better *in*formed; they are to be *trans*formed. This story, says John, carries its own power; and the sign that the power is at work is that those who read the story find themselves caught up

John's Gospel is written to say something about Jesus and something specific to the readers. They are not just to be better informed; they are to be transformed.

The message of John to non-Jewish hearers is, basically, that 'salvation is from the Jews' (4:22). But the very way he has written his book shows that, though it is indeed from the Jews, it is for everyone...

Jesus left Judea and went back once more to Galilee.

Now he had to go through Samaria. So he came to a town in Samaria called Sychar, near the plot of ground Jacob had given to his son Joseph. Jacob's well was there, and Jesus, tired as he was from the journey, sat down by the well. It was about the sixth hour.

When a Samaritan woman came to draw water, Jesus said to her, 'Will you give me a drink?' (His disciples had gone into the town to buy food.)

The Samaritan woman said to him, 'You are a Jew and I am a Samaritan woman. How can you ask me for a drink?' (For Jews do not associate with Samaritans.)

Jesus answered her, 'If you knew the gift of God and who it is that asks you for a drink, you would have asked him and he would have given you living water.'

'Sir,' the woman said, 'you have nothing to draw with and the well is deep. Where can you get this living water? Are you greater than our father Jacob, who gave us the well and drank from it himself, as did also his sons and his flocks and herds?'

Jesus answered, 'Everyone who drinks this water will be thirsty again, but whoever drinks the water I give him will never thirst. Indeed, the water I give him will become in him a spring of water welling up to eternal life.'

The woman said to him, 'Sir, give me this water so that I won't get thirsty and have to keep coming here to draw water.'

He told her, 'Go, call your husband and come back.'

'I have no husband,' she replied.

Jesus said to her, 'You are right when you say you have no husband. The fact is, you have had five husbands, and the man you now have is not your husband. What you have just said is quite true.'

'Sir,' the woman said, 'I can see that you are a prophet. Our fathers worshipped on this mountain, but you Jews claim that the place where we must worship is in Jerusalem.'

Jesus declared, 'Believe me, woman, a time is coming when you will worship the Father neither on this mountain nor in Jerusalem. You Samaritans worship what you do not know; we worship what we do know, for salvation is from the Jews. Yet a time is coming and has now come when the true worshippers will worship the Father in spirit and truth, for they are the kind of worshippers the Father seeks. God is spirit, and his worshippers must worship in spirit and in truth.'

JOHN 4:3–24

within it. They find themselves believing in Jesus. They find this new dimension and quality of life bubbling up inside them (see 4:14; 7:38).

When we study how John has gone about writing his book with this intent, we discover that he has been amazingly sophisticated and astonishingly simple at the same time. The book appears artless, but is in fact a remarkable web of patterns and themes (water, bread, life, light, and so on), all of which cluster round Jesus. The book is Jewish through and through; and yet it is expressed in language which the pagan world, particularly the world of Greek philosophy, would recognize and might resonate with. Of course, the message of John to non-Jewish hearers is, basically, that 'salvation is from the Jews' (4:22). But the very way he has written his book shows that, though it is indeed *from* the Jews, it is *for* everyone. Nineteen centuries have proved him right.

Why Luke?

Luke, too, tells us why he wrote his book. This time the statement comes at the beginning:

> *Since many have undertaken to set down an orderly account of the events that have been fulfilled among us, just as they were handed on to us by those who from the beginning were eye-witnesses and servants of the word, I too decided, after investigating every thing carefully from the very first, to write an orderly account for you, most excellent Theophilus, so that you may know the truth concerning the things about which you have been instructed.*
>
> LUKE 1:1–4

We don't know who 'Theophilus' was, or whether he was already a Christian or not. What we do know is that lots of authors in Luke's world (the world of reasonably cultured and educated people in the first-century Greco-Roman world) wrote books with prefaces rather like this. Some prefaces fairly similar to this are found at the start of serious history books. Some, extremely like this, come at the start of serious works of science. This doesn't of itself prove that Luke was a doctor, an educated scientist, but it certainly puts him on the map of learning and literature. He is presenting Jesus as someone the educated world needs to take seriously.

Well, of course it does. If Luke is right, Jesus is the fulfilment of the Jewish story, which was the focal point of the world's story. Luke tells the story of Jesus' birth as the Prince of Peace, within the empire of Augustus Caesar, who thought *he* was the Prince of Peace. Luke tells the story of Jesus' death at the hands of the Roman empire, suffering a grievous injustice from the system that prided itself precisely on its justice. Small wonder that, in Luke's second volume, the Acts of the Apostles, Paul and his friends get charged with treason, with saying that 'there is another King, namely Jesus' (Acts 17:7). There can only be one king of the world. The Roman Emperor thought it was him. Luke has other ideas.

Ironically, Luke is sometimes supposed to be telling the Roman empire that Christianity is a 'safe' religion, that it's innocent of subversive activity. True, he does want to make it clear that the Roman state has no legal case against Christianity; but that's not because it's simply a private religious activity, or some other figment of late-Western imagination. As far as Luke is concerned, the reason the Roman state should

Caravaggio: 'The Supper at Emmaus'
(Luke 24:13–35)

not object to Christianity is *because it's true*. He wants Theophilus to know the *truth* about the things he's been hearing about.

So we shouldn't be surprised when Luke has Jesus addressing his fellow-Jews in his own home town of Nazareth, and nearly getting lynched for his seditious agenda (Luke 4:16–30). Jesus' kingdom-message, Luke is saying, is so explosive that, even though it's the fulfilment of Israel's hopes, even though it will offer to the world the peace that can come no other way, it will seem deeply threatening to those within both those systems who are bent on organizing the world around their own security or vested interests.

Nor should we be surprised when, at the end of his Gospel, Luke draws the threads together by telling the marvellous story of the two disciples on the road to Emmaus (24:13–27). Jesus, in his death and resurrection, has become the point towards which the whole scriptural story had been moving. Now he is to be known in the breaking of the bread, as the community meets together in his name. But he will not be known only to the little group of close followers. As he says to the disciples: now that the Jewish scriptures have been fulfilled, 'repentance and forgiveness of sins is to be proclaimed in his name to all the nations' (24:47). The whole world needs to know that there is a different way of living, a new way of life—a way characterized by *repentance* and *forgiveness* of wrongdoing, replacing the rule of violence and hatred. I have a suspicion Luke would like to go back and underscore that for the twentieth century, which has seen more violence than any previous one. Those who read Luke's Gospel with both eyes and ears open may discover that they, too, become 'witnesses of these things' (24:48).

Jesus' kingdom-message, Luke is saying, is so explosive that, even though it's the fulfilment of Israel's hopes, even though it will offer to the world the peace that can come no other way, it will seem deeply threatening to those within both those systems who are bent on organizing the world around their own security or vested interests.

Why Matthew?

Matthew is the most obviously Jewish of the Gospels. Yet it is he who stresses most vividly the call of Jesus to the whole world:

All authority in heaven and on earth has been given to me. Go therefore and make disciples of all nations, baptizing them in the name of the Father and of the Son and of the Holy Spirit, and teaching them to obey everything that I have commanded you. And remember, I am with you always, to the end of the age.

MATTHEW 28:18–20

Matthew sees, in Jesus, the fulfilment of the promise of Israel's God to his people. The God who promised that a child would be born whose name will be 'Emmanuel—God with us' (Matthew 1:23, quoting Isaiah 7:14), has now fulfilled that promise: *Jesus* will be 'with you always, even to the end of the age'. Matthew's Gospel is written to tell us who this Jesus is who will be with us, and how the fulfilment of the promise has come about.

Matthew stresses fulfilment of promise, again and again, throughout his Gospel. 'These things took place to fulfil that which was spoken by the prophet...'; this comes almost as a refrain. But he does much more than simply quote scripture and show how Jesus has fulfilled it. He *structures* his work so as to make the same point at a deep level. He organizes the teaching of Jesus into five great blocks, so as to correspond, in form though not in substance, with

Matthew is the most obviously Jewish of the Gospels. Yet it is he who stresses most vividly the call of Jesus to the whole world.

the Five Books of Moses, the 'Pentateuch', which stood at the head of the Jewish scriptures. (The blocks are Matthew 5—7; 10; 13; 18; 23—25.) Jesus, for Matthew, is the new Moses; but he is far more. He is the Messiah, drawing Israel's history to its climax (Matthew 1:2–16), making Herod shiver in his shoes (Matthew 2:1–16). He is the very embodiment of wisdom. He is the Son, who alone reveals the Father (Matthew 11:25–27). He is the Son of man, whose vindication will be manifest when Jerusalem, which has rejected him, is destroyed (Matthew 24).

And he is the one to whom the Gentiles will come in worship and adoration. This was always a vital Jewish theme (see, for instance, Isaiah 49:6–26; Zechariah 8:20–23). Now it is fulfilled in Jesus. The wise men come from the East at his birth (Matthew 2:1–12). The Roman centurion has faith, which points to the time when 'many will come from east and west and eat with Abraham, Isaac and Jacob in the kingdom of heaven' (8:11). The Caananite woman has faith, and her daughter is

healed (15:21–28). And ultimately, as we saw, Jesus sends his disciples out into all the world, over which he now claims authority.

Because Israel is the chosen people of the one true God, the one who draws Israel's scriptures and history together, and fulfills them in his own death and resurrection, is the one whom the true God now sets in authority over the whole cosmos. His followers must go and make disciples, everywhere; God's love reaches out to embrace the whole world. And Matthew's Gospel is written in order to be a key part of

Duccio: 'The Great Commission'
(Matthew 28:16–20)

their equipment as they do so. If we want to read it for all it's worth, we must read it with this in mind: one eye looking back to Jesus, one eye looking out on the world this Jesus claims as his own. That's the way to get Matthew in focus.

Why Mark?

Mark is the shortest, the darkest, the strangest of the Gospels. It's the Gospel for the cynic-in-a-hurry. It tells you the story (Who is Jesus? Why did he die?), sharpened to a point. And it leaves you with the challenge: follow him.

Mark, as we saw, is usually regarded as the earliest of the Gospels, though a sizeable minority of scholars have challenged that. Certainly his book stands very close to Matthew's (almost every story in Mark is in Matthew, though Matthew's versions tend to be shorter); but the relationship between them can be argued either way. Mark's Gospel, however, seems to have quite a different sort of purpose from Matthew's. Matthew presumes that the reader has enough leisure to take in the lengthy discourses, to work out the subtle structure of the book. Mark takes you by the scruff of the neck and tells you, breathlessly, that this is urgent and important and you'd better listen carefully.

He structures his work quite carefully, but, unlike Matthew, quite obviously. The first half of the book leads the reader to ask, long before Jesus puts the question to the disciples explicitly: who is this? By the time Peter faces the question (8:29) the reader is ready to hear the answer: 'You are the Messiah.' You are the king we've been waiting for. You are the one we will follow, the one through whom our God will redeem us at last.

But the second half, which begins at that moment, shows that Peter's grasp of messiahship and what it would mean was only half of the truth. The second half is all about the fact that this Messiah will get to his kingdom through suffering and dying. This is simply not on Peter's (or the other disciples') map of serious options. But for Mark it's the main thing to grasp. What Jesus does in dying on the cross is to establish his kingdom.

Mark is the shortest, the darkest, the strangest of the Gospels. It's the Gospel for the cynic-in-a-hurry... Mark takes you by the scruff of the neck and tells you, breathlessly, that this is urgent and important and you'd better listen carefully.

Who was Mark written for? It's difficult to be precise. But it's quite possible, even likely, that his first audience was a little group of Christians undergoing, or facing the possibility of, persecution and suffering. They needed to know for sure that Jesus really was the Messiah, the true king; they shouldn't look for another Jewish messiah, and they shouldn't regard Caesar as the true Lord of the world. They were bound to be rejected by non-Christian Jews, and by Caesar's henchmen. They must hold fast to Jesus, and to him alone.

FACING PAGE
Fouquet: 'The Arrest of Jesus' This illumination for a Book of Hours shows a soldier ripping a cloak from a young man fleeing from the scene (top left). The incident occurs only in Mark's Gospel *(14:51)*, which could suggest that Mark himself was the young man, and therefore an eye-witness of the events.

Jesus, the true king, however, had gone to his enthronement ceremony on the cross. It was quite on the cards that they would be summoned to follow him. This is the most deeply subversive message the world can face, because it looks at the ultimate sanction that the world can hold over people who refuse to toe the line and, instead of submitting to such blackmail, embraces even suffering and death as falling within the saving purposes of God.

John's Gospel is designed to bring you to your knees in wonder, love and praise. Luke's is meant to make you sit up and think hard about Jesus as Lord of the whole world. Matthew's is like a beautifully bound book which the Christian must study and ponder at leisure, steadily reordering one's life in the process. Mark's is like a hastily printed revolutionary tract, stuffed into a back pocket, and frequently pulled out, read by torchlight, and whispered to one's co-conspirators. You need all four. You never know when you are going to have to call on them.

John's Gospel is designed to bring you to your knees in wonder, love and praise. Luke's is meant to make you sit up and think hard about Jesus as Lord of the whole world. Matthew's is like a beautifully bound book which the Christian must study and ponder at leisure. Mark's is like a hastily printed revolutionary tract., read by torchlight, and whispered to one's co-conspirators.

Reading the Gospels for yourself

So how do we read and use the Gospels? There's much that could be said at this point, but let me sum up by making four brief suggestions.

□ First, read the Gospels from cover to cover, struggling to make more and more sense of exactly who Jesus was. Don't assume you know exactly who he was, what it was like to be that first-century Jew from Nazareth who believed he had a vocation to act as Israel's Messiah, to die on a Roman cross, and so to save the world. Expect to have to revise your picture of Jesus, of his aims and intentions, of the subtlety and power of his vision, of his teasing riddles and world-changing parables, and, indeed, to have to revise it over and over again. The Gospels will help you do that if you let them, if you are truly open to hearing and learning new things which you hadn't grasped before.

Expect to have to revise your picture of Jesus, of his aims and intentions, of the subtlety and power of his vision, of his teasing riddles and world-changing parables, and, indeed, to have to revise it over and over again.

Sometimes some modern secondary literature may help. If you're already familiar with the Gospels and the stories they contain, it may be genuinely hard for you to see behind 'what you've always thought this story meant', and view it in its true first-century context. Some of the books in the bibliography may help you in this fascinating and challenging quest.

□ Second, read the Gospels from cover to cover, struggling with each book to see what each evangelist is saying as a whole. Think into the situation of his likely first readers: small groups of struggling Christians, living in the two worlds of Judaism and paganism and yet now belonging truly to neither, standing over against both with a message of love and salvation which both groups are (paradoxically) going to find deeply threatening.

della Francesca: 'The Resurrection'

Enjoy, and get to know, the distinctive way that each evangelist has both of organizing his material and of shaping it. You might get hold of a synopsis in which the Gospels are laid out side by side, so that you can compare them easily; or you may just enjoy reading one of them with bookmarks in the others to flick over to the parallel passages.

Incidentally, if you don't know any Greek, do make sure that you have at least two modern translations to compare. Ancient Greek and modern Western languages don't easily fit into each other, and in many passages you will be surprised how much difference there may be between versions.

□ Third, read the Gospels from cover to cover, struggling to ask another question. If this Jesus really did draw together the threads of the saving plan of the one true God; if on the cross, and in his resurrection, he really did deal with evil once and for all; if the people who read his story now, and make it their own, have the responsibility to implement his victory over evil in the world: then *how can people, today, retell the story so that the world gets the message*?

How can these explosive documents become once more the world-shaking thing they always were, so that the Caesars and Herods and Pilates and Caiaphases of our own world and our own day shake in their shoes as they hear about the Prince of Peace, the King of Kings?

If we don't read the Gospels with this question in mind, we are bound, ultimately, to distort them.

> *Put yourself into the story and see what happens. Take your time. Imagine the scene. Listen as Jesus speaks to the person in the story; then stop the movie and insert a fresh scene, this time including yourself.*

□ But, fourth, read the Gospels from cover to cover, slowly, carefully and thoughtfully, wondering throughout: if I were in the crowd at that scene, what would Jesus say to me? If I were the person lying on the stretcher, what might happen to me? If I were one of the critics, carping and objecting to Jesus, how would he react? If I were one of the soldiers nailing Jesus to the cross, how would he look at me? If I were his mother... his brother... his sister... If I were his disciple...

In other words, *put yourself into the story and see what happens*. Take your time. Imagine the scene. Listen as Jesus speaks to the person in the story; then stop the movie and insert a fresh scene, this time including yourself. Tell him how you feel, what you're thinking, why you're angry or sad, what you're frightened of (notice how often he says 'Don't be afraid').

When you've said your piece, don't rush on or run away. Pause; wait; slow down; be quiet; and listen. Even to hear the silence, and to know that Jesus is there in it, is more than worth the effort; but you may hear something else as well.

And when you do, remember the wise words of Jesus' mother Mary to the servants in John 2:5: 'Whatever he says to you, do it.'

Further Reading

If you want a quick overview of what's been happening in Jesus-studies these last few years, you might try Stephen Neill and Tom Wright, *The Interpretation of the New Testament, 1861–1986*, pp. 379–403. A lot of the following books have a section on 'the story so far'. See too my article in *The Anchor Bible Dictionary*, vol. 3. The *ABD*, incidentally, has a lot of excellent things in all areas, though like all multi-author works it is, of course, uneven.

Bammel, E.; Moule, C. F. D. (eds.) 1984. *Jesus and the Politics of his Day*. Cambridge: CUP

Major collection of articles by (mostly) world ranking scholars. A response to Brandon (see below), but of much wider significance.

Barton, Stephen A. 1992. *The Spirituality of the Gospels*. London: SPCK/Peabody: Hendrickson.

A very worthwhile study of the Gospels, suggesting ways of reading them to bring out their theological and spiritual insights.

Betz, Otto. 1968 [1965]. *What Do We Know About Jesus?* Trans. M. Kohl. London: SCM Press/Philadelphia: Westminster.

Short, pithy, readable, historically sensitive. Betz was making good use of Jewish material (for example the Scrolls), in the attempt to reconstruct the history of Jesus, some while before the majority of the scholarly world woke up to this task.

Bockmuehl, Markus. 1994. *This Jesus: Martyr, Lord, Messiah*. Edinburgh: T & T Clark.

A rising young star in New Testament Studies, Bockmuehl (of Cambridge University, England) engages in a refreshing way with recent writing, and comes up with a striking portrait of Jesus.

Borg, Marcus J. 1984. *Conflict, Holiness and Politics in the Teachings of Jesus*. Studies in the Bible and Early Christianity, vol. 5. New York/Toronto: Edwin Mellen Press.

Borg's first, and in some ways foundational, book about Jesus. It remains extremely important.

——. 1987. *Jesus: A New Vision*. San Francisco: Harper and Row.

A more reflective account, making Borg's scholarship more widely accessible.

Brandon, S. G. F. 1967. *Jesus and the Zealots: A Study of the Political Factor in Primitive Christianity*.

Manchester: Manchester University Press/New York: Scribner.

The one that put the cat among the pigeons. Brandon's argument (that Jesus was basically a 'zealot', a Jewish freedom-fighter, and that the early church hushed this up), wasn't new in itself. But it sparked off fierce debates which still rumble on in different forms.

Brown, Colin. 1984. *Miracles and the Critical Mind*. Grand Rapids, Mich.: Eerdmans.

——. 1988 [1985]. *Jesus in European Protestant Thought, 1778–1860*. Grand Rapids: Baker.

Brown is a philosopher and historian who has become increasingly involved in Jesus-research. These are important treatments which deserve taking very seriously—as does his major work on Jesus, due out in the not too distant future.

Brown, Raymond E. 1994. *The Death of the Messiah: From Gethsemane to the Grave. A Commentary on the Passion Narratives in the Four Gospels*. Anchor Bible Reference Library. New York and London: Doubleday and Geoffrey Chapman.

Massive, hugely learned, yet clear and accessible. This will be a landmark for at least a generation. If he's right, the 'Jesus Seminar' are completely mistaken about a great deal; which is perhaps why Crossan has at once written a stiff reply (1995).

Burridge, Richard A. 1992. *What are the Gospels? A Comparison with Graeco-Roman Biography*. Cambridge: CUP.

——. 1994 *Four Gospels, One Jesus? A Symbolic Reading*. London: SPCK/Grand Rapids: Eerdmans.

Burridge is a classicist turned New Testament scholar. His earlier work demonstrates that the four Gospels really are 'biographies'; his later one is a more popular introduction.

Caird, G. B. 1963. The Gospel of St. Luke. Harmondsworth: Penguin/Philadelphia: Westminster.

——. 1965. *Jesus and the Jewish Nation*. London: Athlone Press.

——. 1980. *The Language and Imagery of the Bible*. London: Duckworth/Grand Rapids: Eerdmans (1996).

Caird was one of the most lucid and crisp writers in the field. He saw clearly, thirty years ago, issues that are only now coming to the fore. His work on language and imagery is basic to a correct understanding of various issues, particularly the meaning of 'apocalyptic'.

Chilton, Bruce D. 1992. *The Temple of Jesus: His Sacrificial Program Within a Cultural History of Sacrifice*. University Park, Pa.: Pennsylvania State UP.

Chilton has studied an important and often neglected part of Jesus' Jewish context, namely the rabbinic 'Targums' (scripture commentaries). From this, he argues that when Jesus said 'kingdom of God' he meant 'God himself in strength'. His book on the temple is a major, important (and sometimes quite dense) attempt to think through how sacrifice 'works' culturally, and what Jesus was trying to do in opposing the sacrificial cult in the temple.

Crossan, J. Dominic. 1991. *The Historical Jesus: The Life of a Mediterranean Jewish Peasant*. Edinburgh and San Francisco: T & T Clark; Harper.

——, ed. 1991 [1986]. *Jesus Parallels: A Workbook for the Jesus Tradition*. 2nd ed. [1st ed. entitled *Sayings Parallels*] Philadelphia: Fortress.

——. 1994. *Jesus: A Revolutionary Biography*. San Francisco: HarperSanFrancisco.

——. 1995. *Who Killed Jesus? Exposing the Roots of Anti-Semitism in the Gospel Story of the Death of Jesus*. San Francisco: HarperSanFrancisco.

Crossan vies with Sanders for the position of the leading North American Jesus-scholar of today. His major book on Jesus (1991) sets out his position in full; his smaller one (1994) presents it at a more popular level; his third one (1995) replies to Raymond Brown (see above), arguing that the Passion narratives in the canonical Gospels are theologically motivated fictions with a strong strand of anti-semitism. Instead, Crossan thinks we can find the original passion narrative within the 'Gospel of Peter' (see 1988), which almost all other scholars think is a much later work.

Davis, Stephen T. 1993. *Risen Indeed: Making Sense of the Resurrection*. London: SPCK/Grand Rapids: Eerdmans.

A recent work on the resurrection by a philosopher, arguing strongly for the historicity of Jesus' bodily resurrection and of the empty tomb.

Evans, Craig A. 1989. *Life of Jesus Research: An Annotated Bibliography*. Leiden: Brill/

A massive list, containing enough to keep even the most zealous reader busy for a long time. Fortunately, by no means all of the writing catalogued here is of great importance.

Farmer, W. R. 1956. *Maccabees, Zealots and Josephus: An Enquiry Into Jewish Nationalism in the Greco-Roman Period*. New York: Columbia UP.

——. 1964. *The Synoptic Problem: A Critical Analysis*. London, New York: Macmillan.

——. 1982. *Jesus and the Gospel*. Philadelphia: Fortress.

——. 1994. *The Gospel of Jesus: The Pastoral Relevance of the Synoptic Problem*. Louisville: Westminster/John Knox.

Farmer saw, in the 1950s, things that it has taken everyone else thirty years to catch up with. His 1956 book remains important, filled out further by 1982. 1994 reveals some of the subtexts under recent research on the Gospels; Farmer has long advocated, against the mainstream, the priority of Matthew (esp. 1964).

Freyne, Sean. 1988. *Galilee, Jesus and the Gospels: Literary Approaches and Historical Investigations*. Philadelphia: Fortress Press.

The leading light on Galilee at the time of Jesus. Freyne's scholarship must be taken deeply seriously.

Funk, Robert W., and Roy W. Hoover. 1993. *The Five Gospels: The Search for the Authentic Words of Jesus*. New York: Macmillan.

Presents the results of the Jesus Seminar's work in a multi-coloured text, with comments all through which reveal only too clearly the threadbare arguments employed in reaching the conclusions.

Harvey, Anthony E. 1982. *Jesus and the Constraints of History: The Bampton Lectures, 1980*. London: Duckworth.

Important and innovative treatment by a classicist turned theologian. Despite some questionable conclusions, this book remains very significant, though often neglected in recent N. American work.

Hengel, Martin. 1981 [1968]. *The Charismatic Leader and His Followers*. Trans. James Grieg. New York: Crossroad Publishing.

——. 1995. *Studies in Early Christology*. Edinburgh: T & T Clark.

Two very important, sometimes quite technical, books by the most massively learned of current New Testament scholars. He grounds Jesus and early Christology firmly within first-century Judaism.

Horsley, Richard A. 1987. *Jesus and the Spiral of Violence: Popular Jewish Resistance in Roman Palestine*. San Francisco: Harper and Row.

Horsley, Richard A., and John S. Hanson. 1985. *Bandits, Prophets and Messiahs: Popular Movements at the Time of Jesus*. Minneapolis: Winston Press.

Jesus advocated social, not political, revolution, in line with other movements from the poorer end of the social scale.

Johnson, Luke T. 1995. *The Real Jesus*. San Francisco: Harper.

Deeply critical of the 'Jesus Seminar' and a good deal else besides. Argues for a moderate compromise between the older Catholic position (the quest for the historical Jesus is a Protestant problem) and the older existential position (the real Jesus is the one we worship as the risen Lord). Deep scholarship worn very lightly; ultimately not quite satisfying to this reader.

Meier, John P. 1991/4. *A Marginal Jew: Rethinking the Historical Jesus*. Vol. 1. *The Roots of the Problem and the Person*. Vol. 2. *Mentor, Message and Miracles*. New York: Doubleday.

Massive study with roots in modern (as opposed to postmodern) methods of criticism, and results that are substantially conservative. Will be widely used and discussed for years to come. Whether it will advance the subject remains to be seen; but it will form, for many, a solid boulder in the way of the 'Jesus Seminar' and all its works.

Meyer, Ben F. 1979. *The Aims of Jesus*. London: SCM Press.

If I had to choose one book from this list to take to a desert island, it might well be this one. Meyer is the unsung hero of this field—even though I disagree with him on some vital issues. Everything he writes is worth taking very seriously.

Moule, C.F.D. 1967. *The Phenomenon of the New Testament: An Inquiry Into the Implications of Certain Features of the New Testament*. SBT 2nd series, vol. 1. London: SCM Press/ Naperville, Illinois: Allenson.

——. 1977. *The Origin of Christology*. Cambridge: CUP.

The doyen of English NT scholars: two of his most important books.

Riches, John K. 1980. *Jesus and the Transformation of Judaism*. London: Darton, Longman and Todd/New York: Seabury.

An important, though somewhat uneven, work.

Sanders, E.P. 1985. *Jesus and Judaism*. Philadelphia/London: Fortress Press/SCM Press.

——. 1993. *The Historical Figure of Jesus*. London: Penguin.

Probably the most influential NT scholar in the English-speaking world. Very different position to Crossan and the 'Jesus Seminar'. His 1993 book is a good place to start.

Schweitzer, Albert. 1954 [1906]. *The Quest of the Historical Jesus: A Critical Study of Its Progress from Reimarus to Wrede*. Trans. W.B.D. Montgomery. 3rd ed. London: A & C Black/New York: Collier (1968).

The book that brought the 'Old Quest' to an end, and introduced the twentieth century to a fresh reading of the problem. Still enormously worth reading, not least because Schweitzer was a brilliant writer.

Stanton, Graham N. 1989. *The Gospels and Jesus*. Oxford: OUP.

——. 1995. *Gospel Truth? New Light on Jesus and the Gospels*. London: HarperCollins/Valley Forge: Trinity Press International.

1989: A safe and sound book by a safe and sound scholar; a trifle unexciting and unadventurous. 1995: more readable, and takes on some recent theories (especially those of Thiede), coming up with some fresh insights of Stanton's own.

Theissen, Gerd. 1978 [1977]. *Sociology of Early Palestinian Christianity*. [English title: *The First Followers of Jesus*.Trans. J. Bowden. London: SCM Press/ Philadelphia: Fortress.

An early attempt to set the primitive Jesus movement into its sociological context. Quite influential.

——. 1987 [1986]. *The Shadow of the Galilean: The Quest of the Historical Jesus in Narrative Form*. Trans. John Bowden. London: SCM Press/Philadelphia: Fortress.

Brilliant and creative novel-like work. Enormously stimulating, witty, clever and thought-provoking.

——. 1991 [1989]. *The Gospels in Context: Social and Political History in the Synoptic Tradition*. Trans. Linda M. Maloney. Minneapolis: Augsburg Fortress.

Creative look at fresh possibilities in deciding how the materials in the synoptic Gospels became shaped the way they are. Totally different, and far more scholarly, perspective from that offered by the 'Jesus Seminar'.

Thiede, Carsten. 1995. *Rekindling the Word: In Search of Gospel Truth.*

——. and D'Ancona, Matthew. 1996. *The Jesus Papyrus*. London: Weidenfeld & Nicolson.

The books which claim that the Magdalen Papyrus is dated to the first century; that a fragment from Qumran's Cave 7 is part of Mark's Gospel; and that there is something of a scholarly conspiracy to keep all this hushed up.

Vermes, Geza. 1973. *Jesus the Jew: A Historian's Reading of the Gospels*. London: Collins/Philadelphia: Fortress.

——. 1983. *Jesus and the World of Judaism*. London: SCM Press/ Philadelphia: Fortress.

——. 1993. *The Religion of Jesus the Jew*. London: SCM/ Philadelphia: Fortress.

When *Jesus the Jew* came out in 1973, the title itself was somewhat shocking. That it isn't so now is due not least to these solid books by one of the leading scholars of the generation.

Wenham, David. 1989. *The Parables of Jesus: Pictures of Revolution*. London: Hodder & Stoughton/Downers Grove: InterVarsity.

Good popular-level introduction to the parables, bringing out something of their political dimension while never downplaying the theology.

Witherington, Ben. 1990. *The Christology of Jesus*. Minneapolis: Fortress.

——. 1994. *Jesus the Sage: the Pilgrimage of Wisdom*. Minneapolis: Fortress.

——. 1995. *The Jesus Quest: The Third Search for the Jew of Nazareth*. Downer's Grove, Ill.: IVP.

Solid works by a younger conservative scholar; their influence is yet to be felt fully. The 1995 book is a helpful survey.

Wright, N. T. 1992a. *Christian Origins and the Question of God*. Vol. 1. *The New Testament and the People of God*. London, Minneapolis: SPCK, Fortress.

A methodological and historical groundwork for understanding the NT, especially the Gospels and Jesus.

——. 1992b. "Quest for the Historical Jesus". In *The Anchor Bible Dictionary*, ed. David N. Freedman, vol. 3, pp.796–802. New York: Doubleday.

Quick survey of the 'Quest'.

——. 1992c. *Who Was Jesus?* London, Grand Rapids, Mich.: SPCK, Eerdmans.

An answer to Thiering, Wilson and Spong, with a brief historical opening and even briefer concluding positive statement.

——. 1995. "Five Gospels but No Gospel: Jesus and the Seminar". In Farmer 1995, *Crisis in Christology: Essays in Quest of Resolution*. Livonia, Michigan: Dove Booksellers. pp.115–157.

A critique of Funk and Hoover 1993, exposing the shallow and unhistorical arguments used to support the conclusions of the 'Jesus Seminar'.

——. 1996. *Christian Origins and the Question of God.* Vol 2. *Jesus and the Victory of God.* London, Minneapolis: SPCK, Fortress.

A full-scale historical portrait of Jesus within his historical context, interacting in detail with contemporary scholarship.

Yoder, John H. 1972. *The Politics of Jesus: Vicit Agnus Noster*. Grand Rapids: Eerdmans (new edition 1994).

Leading Mennonite argues for Jesus' agenda of non-violence. Still a fascinating read more than twenty years later.

Index

Picture Acknowledgments

Pages 2/3, 10, 12/13 Jon Arnold
Page 14 Lion Publishing/David Alexander
Pages 17, 19 Jon Arnold
Page 22 Lion Publishing/David Townsend
Pages 24/25, 26 Jon Arnold
Page 27 Lion Publishing/David Townsend
Page 28a Lion Publishing/David Alexander
Page 28b Jon Arnold
Pages 30, 33 Lion Publishing/David Alexander
Pages 34, 37, 44 Lion Publishing/David Townsend
Pages 46/47, 48, 50 Lion Publishing/David Alexander
Pages 52/53 Lion Publishing/David Townsend
Page 54 Lion Publishing
Page 56 Lion Publishing/David Townsend
Page 57 Lion Publishing/David Alexander
Pages 58/59, 62, 66, 69 Jon Arnold
Page 73 Lion Publishing/David Townsend
Page 76 Lion Publishing/David Alexander
Pages 77, 80/81 Società Scala, Firenze
Pages 84/85 Reproduced by courtesy of the Trustees, The National Gallery, London
Page 86 Lion Publishing
Page 88 The Board of Trinity College Dublin
Page 90 Lion Publishing/David Alexander
Page 93 Società Scala, Firenze
Pages 96/97 Reproduced by courtesy of the Trustees, The National Gallery, London
Page 107 By courtesy of the board of trustees of the Victoria & Albert Museum
Page 110 Lion Publishing/David Alexander
Page 113 Lion Publishing
Page 122 Società Scala, Firenze
Page 126 Lion Publishing
Pages 131, 134 R.J.L. Smith of Much Wenlock
Pages 136/137 Reproduced by courtesy of the Trustees, The National Gallery, London
Page 139 R.J.L. Smith of Much Wenlock
Page 140 Società Scala, Firenze
Page 142 R.J.L. Smith of Much Wenlock
Page 145 Lauros-Giraudon
Page 147 Società Scala, Firenze